Neo Mandalas
Coloring Book for Adults

by Asma Zergui

ISBN-13:
978-1508537519

ISBN-10:
1508537518

DEDICATION

This artwork is dedicated to my beloved daughter Jasmine,
you are the light that is guiding me .

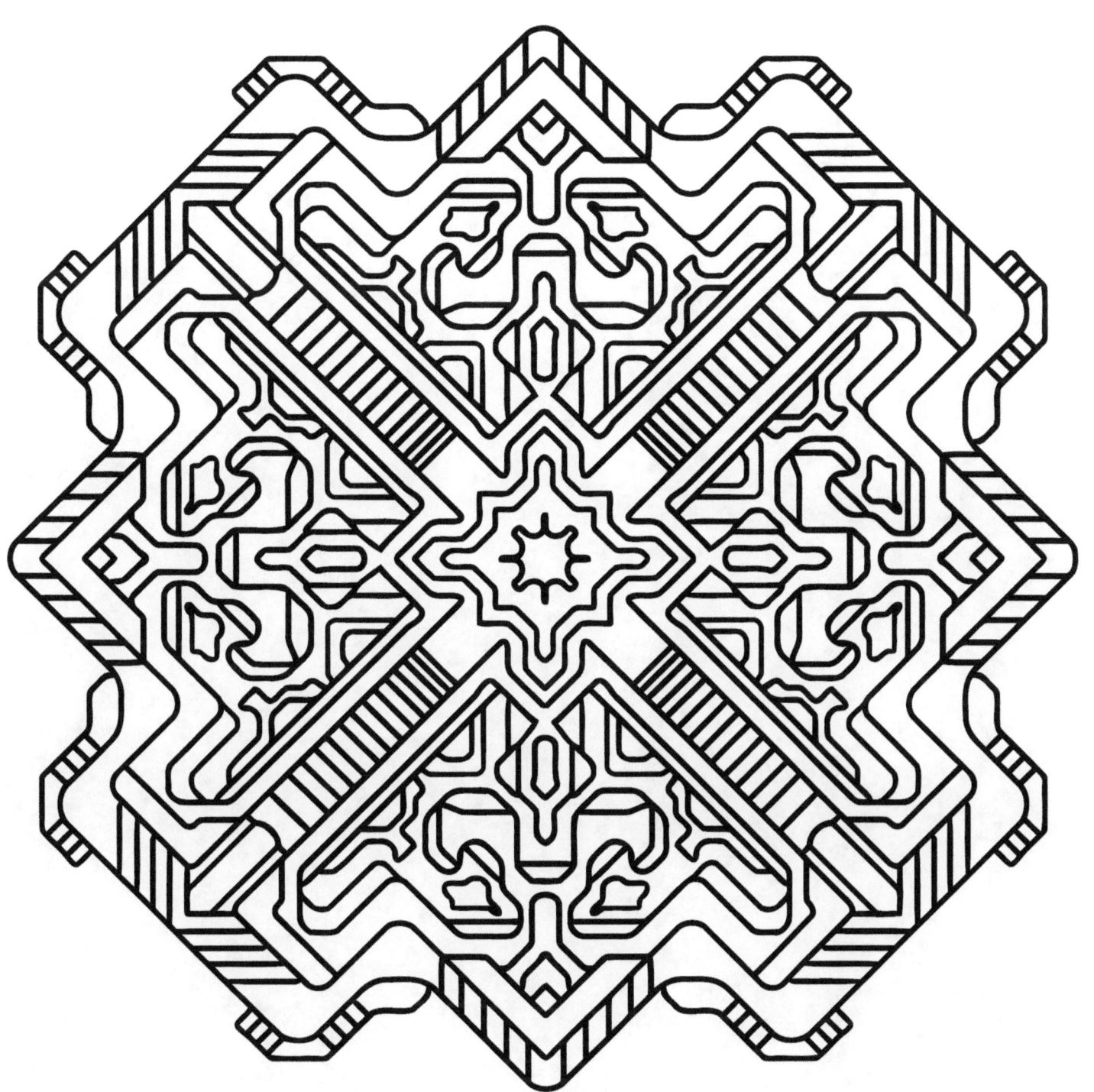

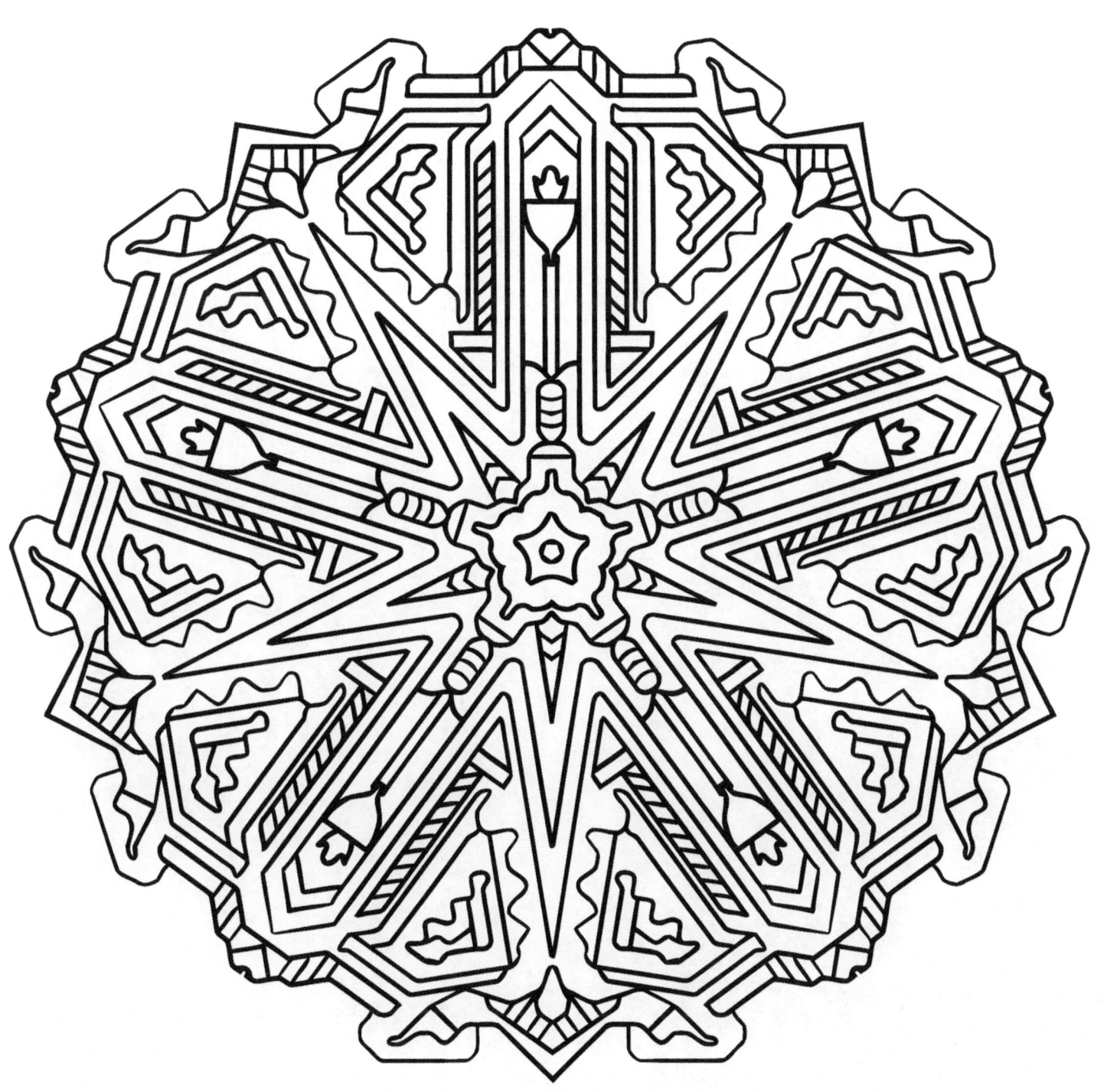

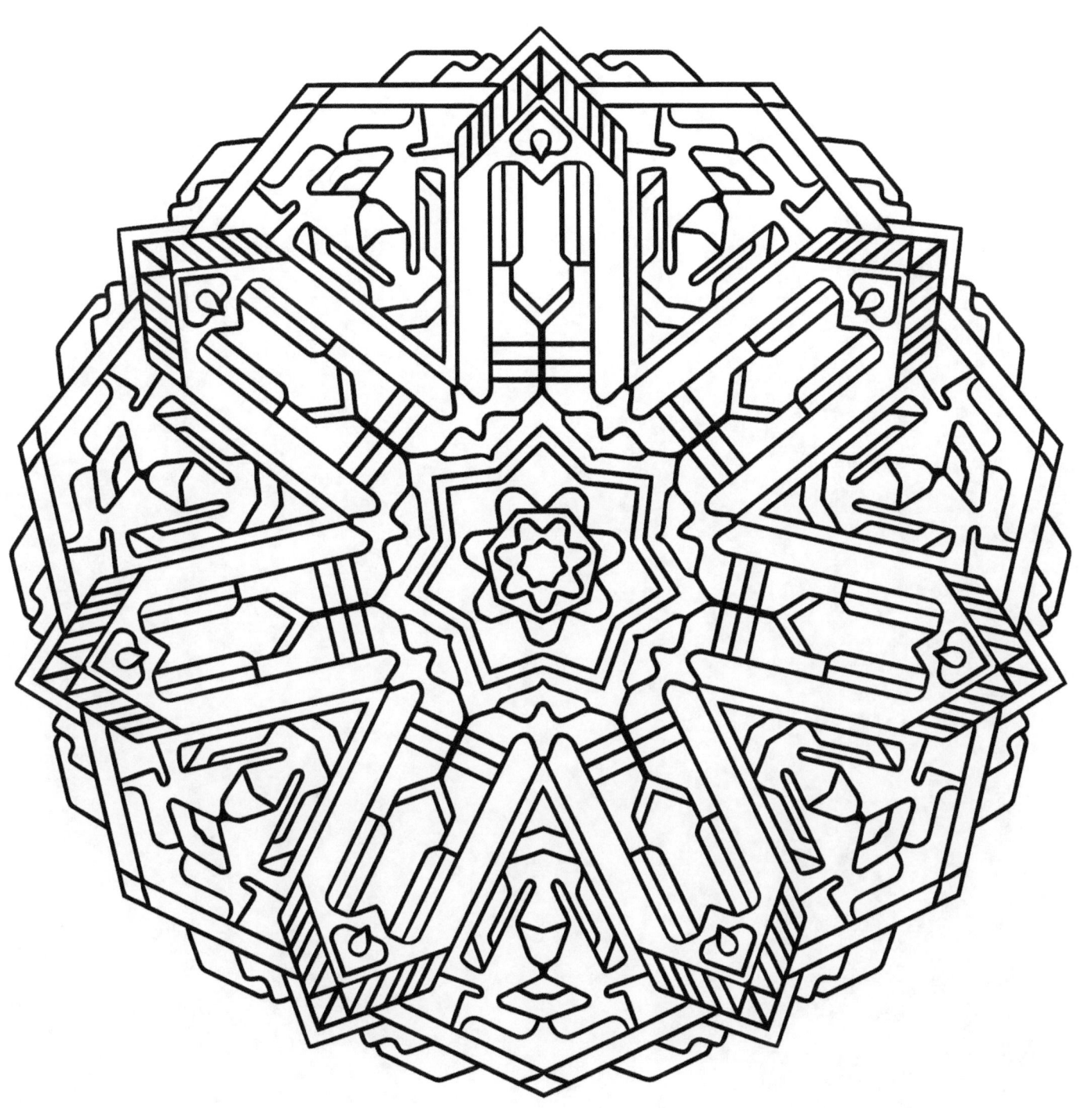

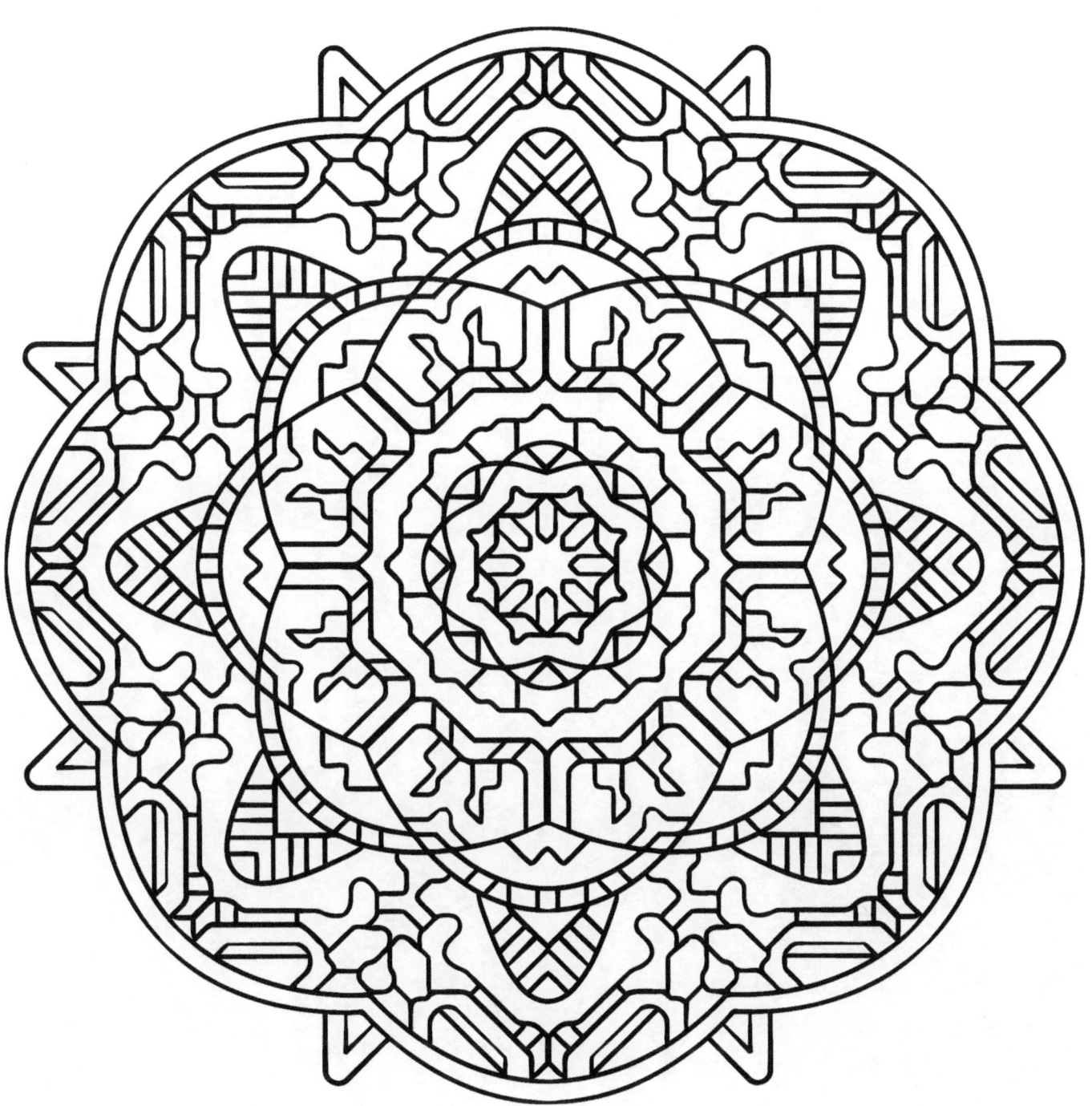

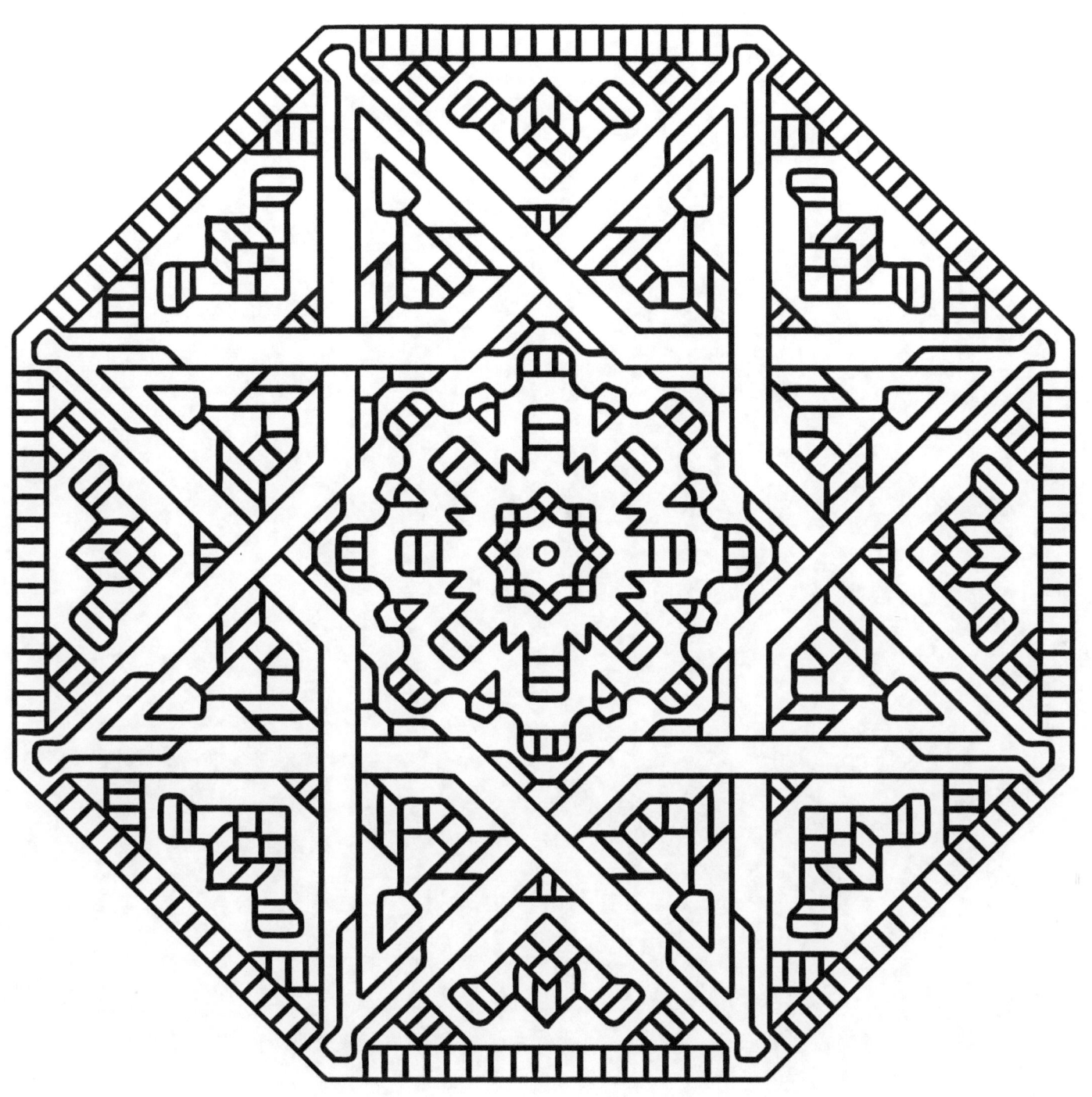

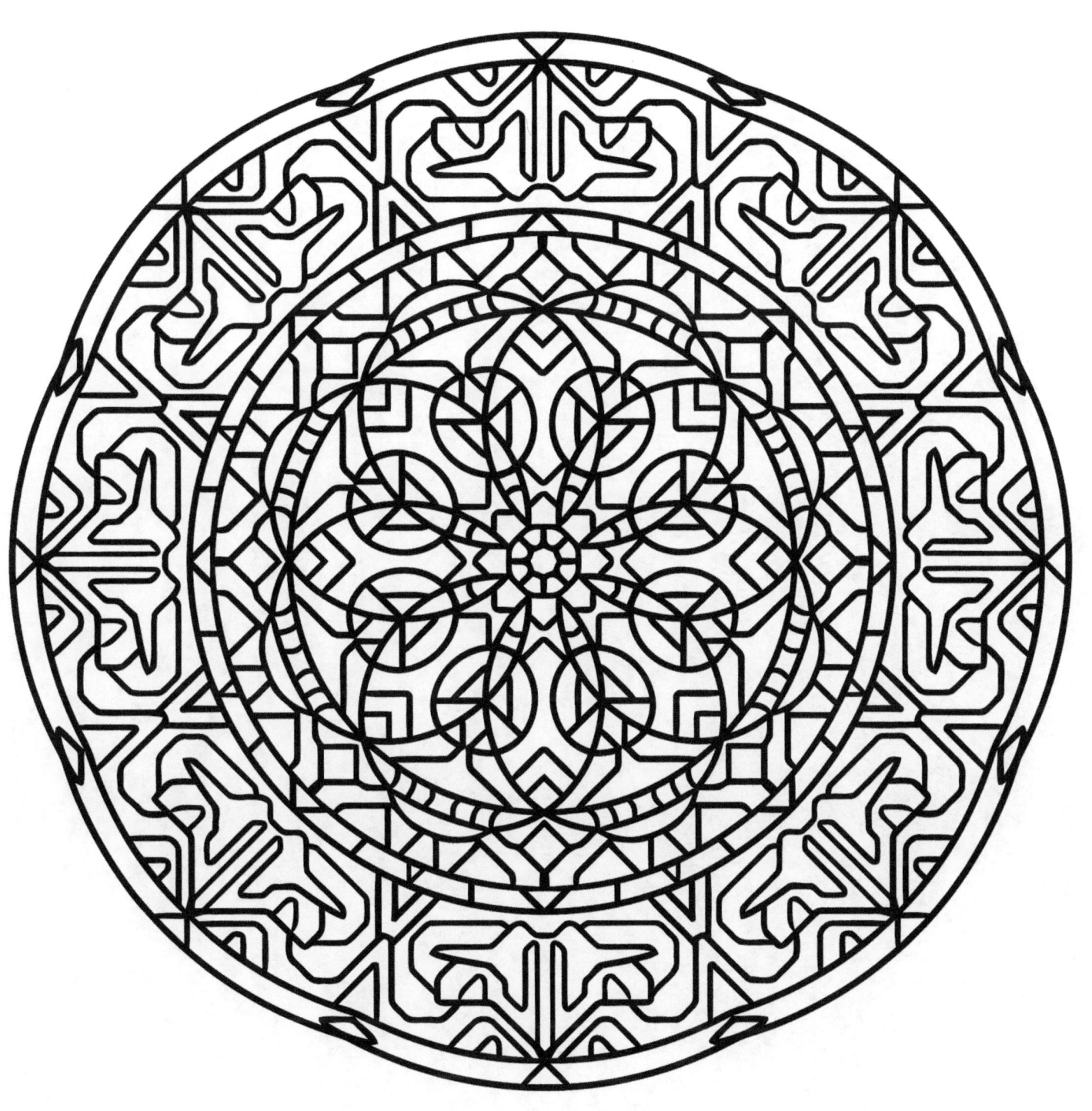

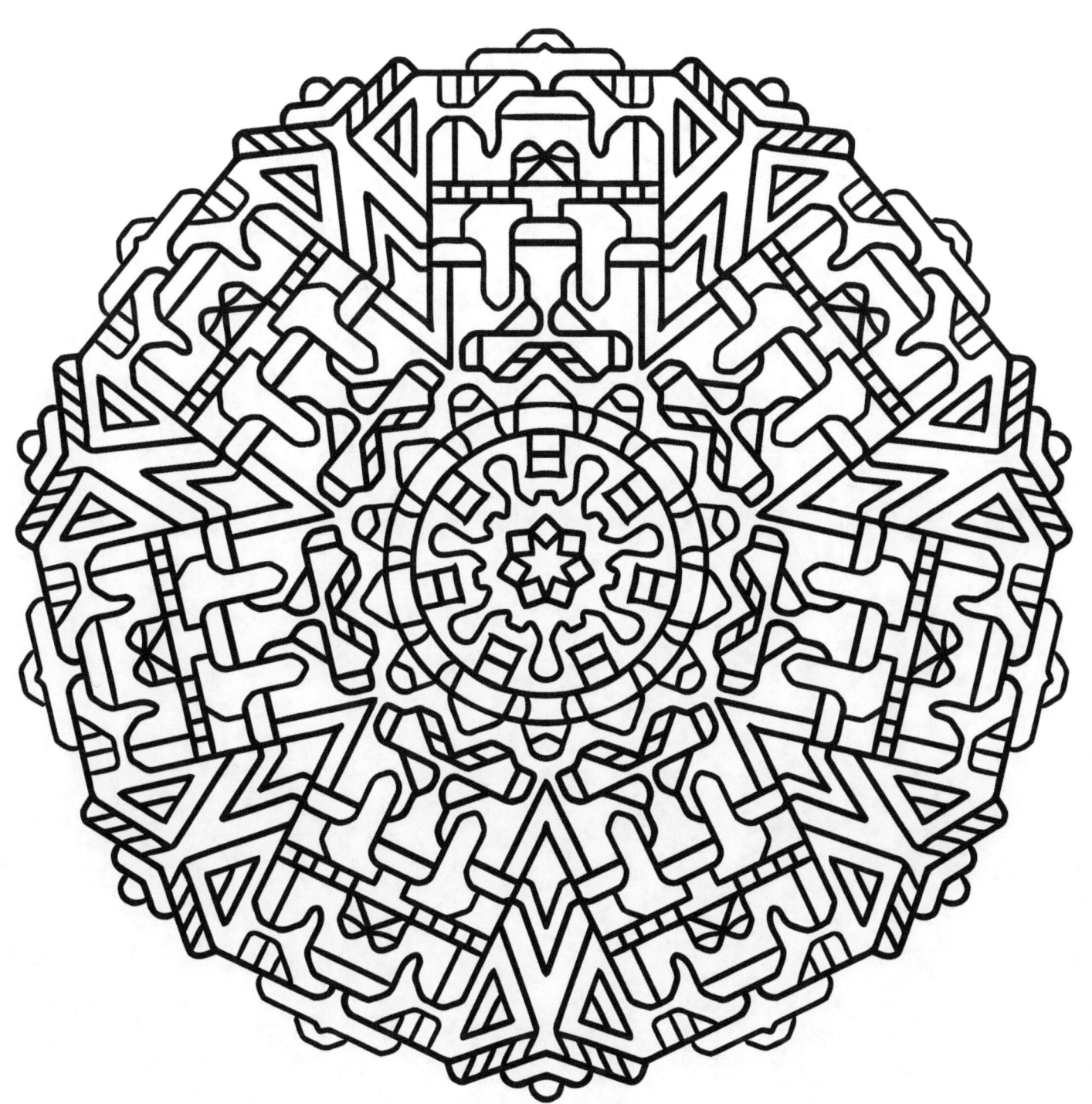

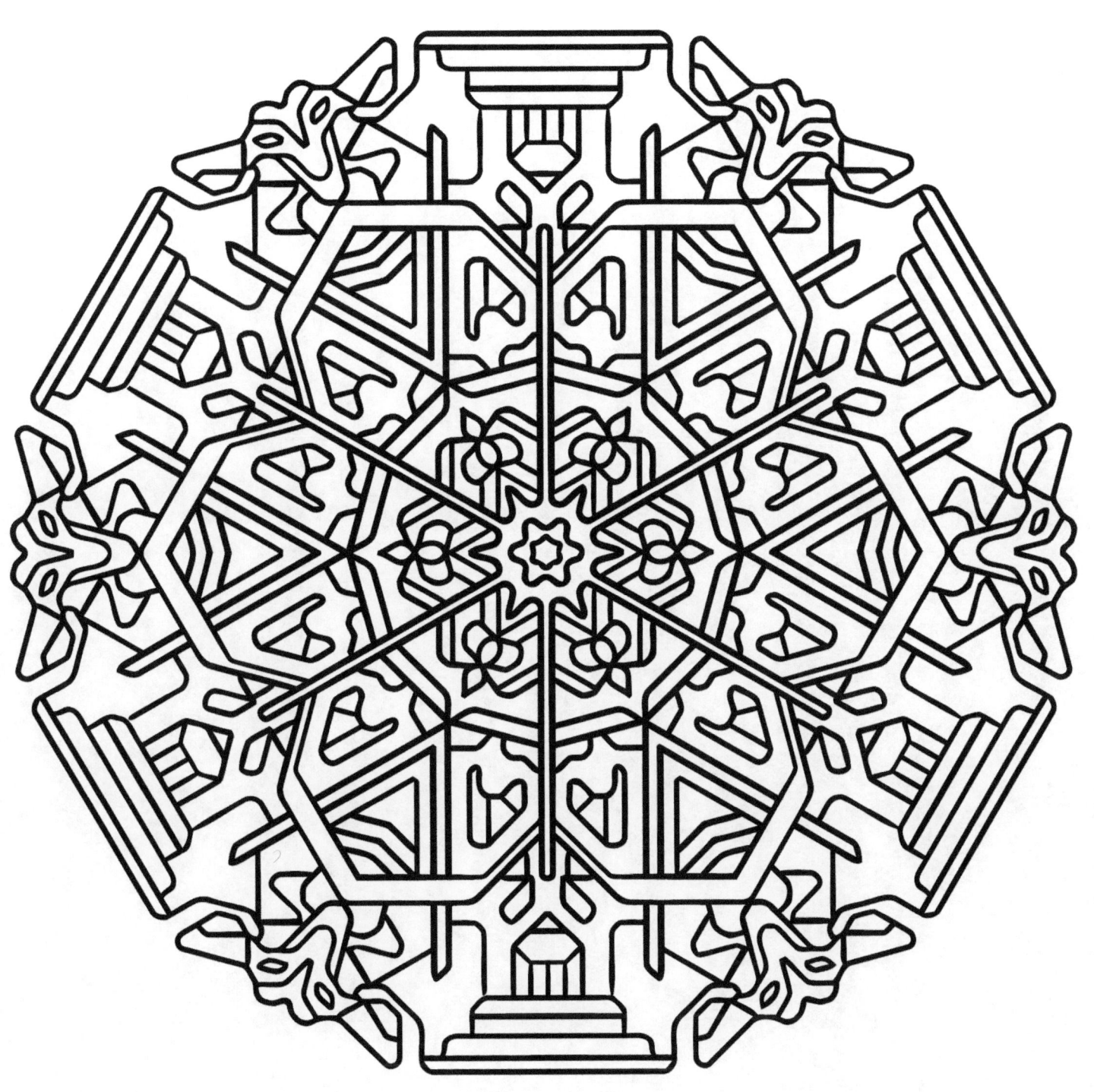

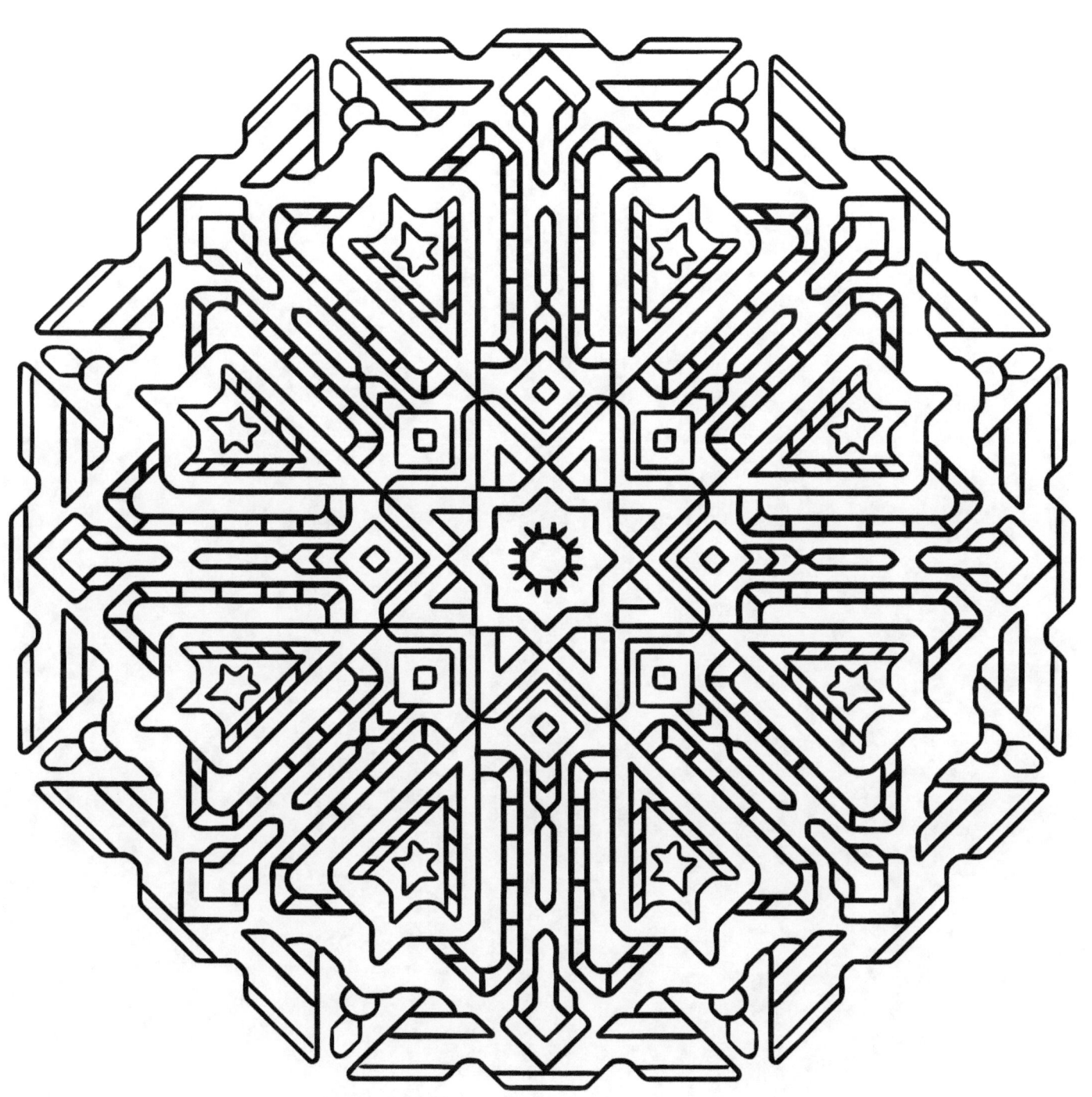

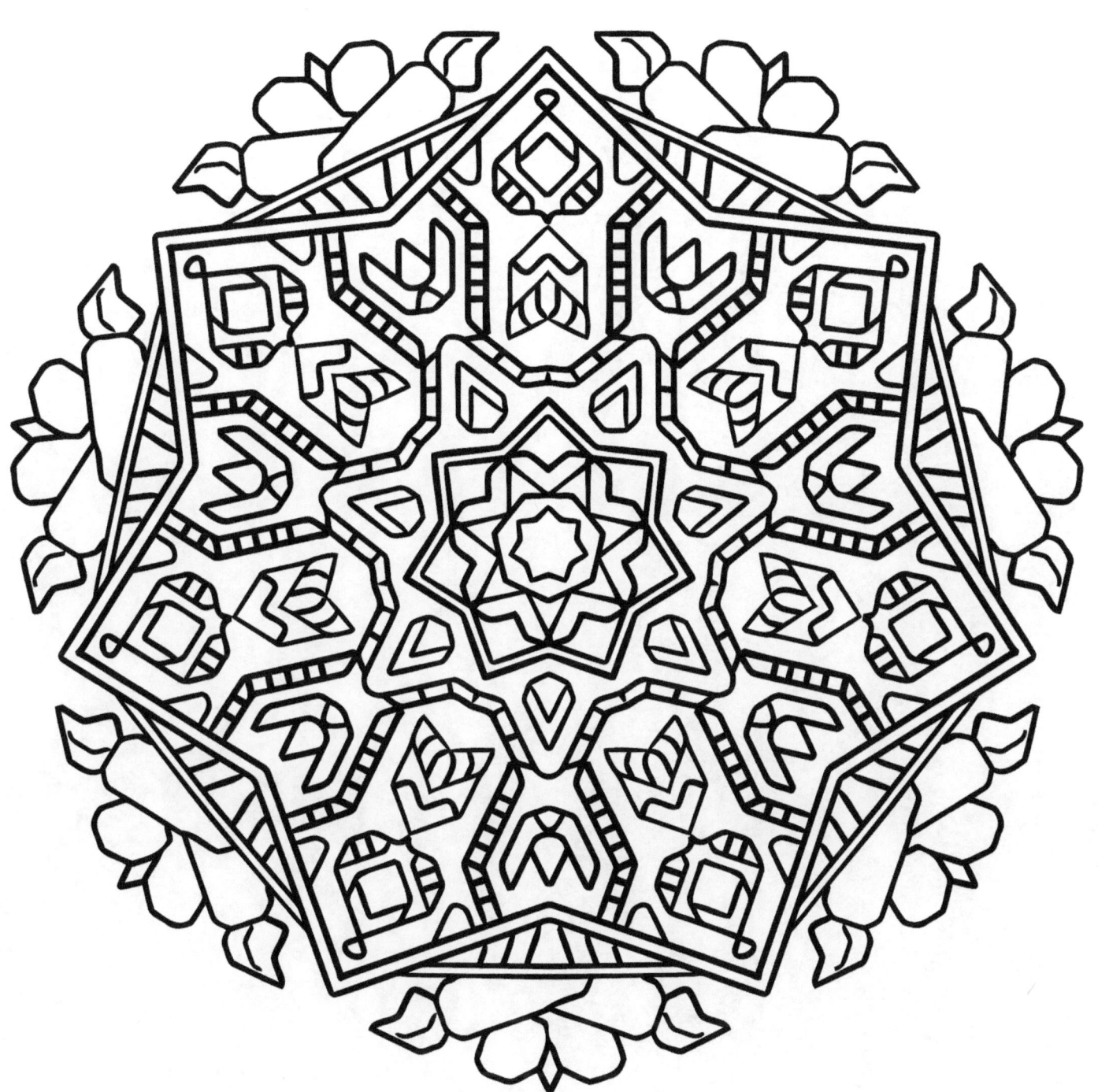

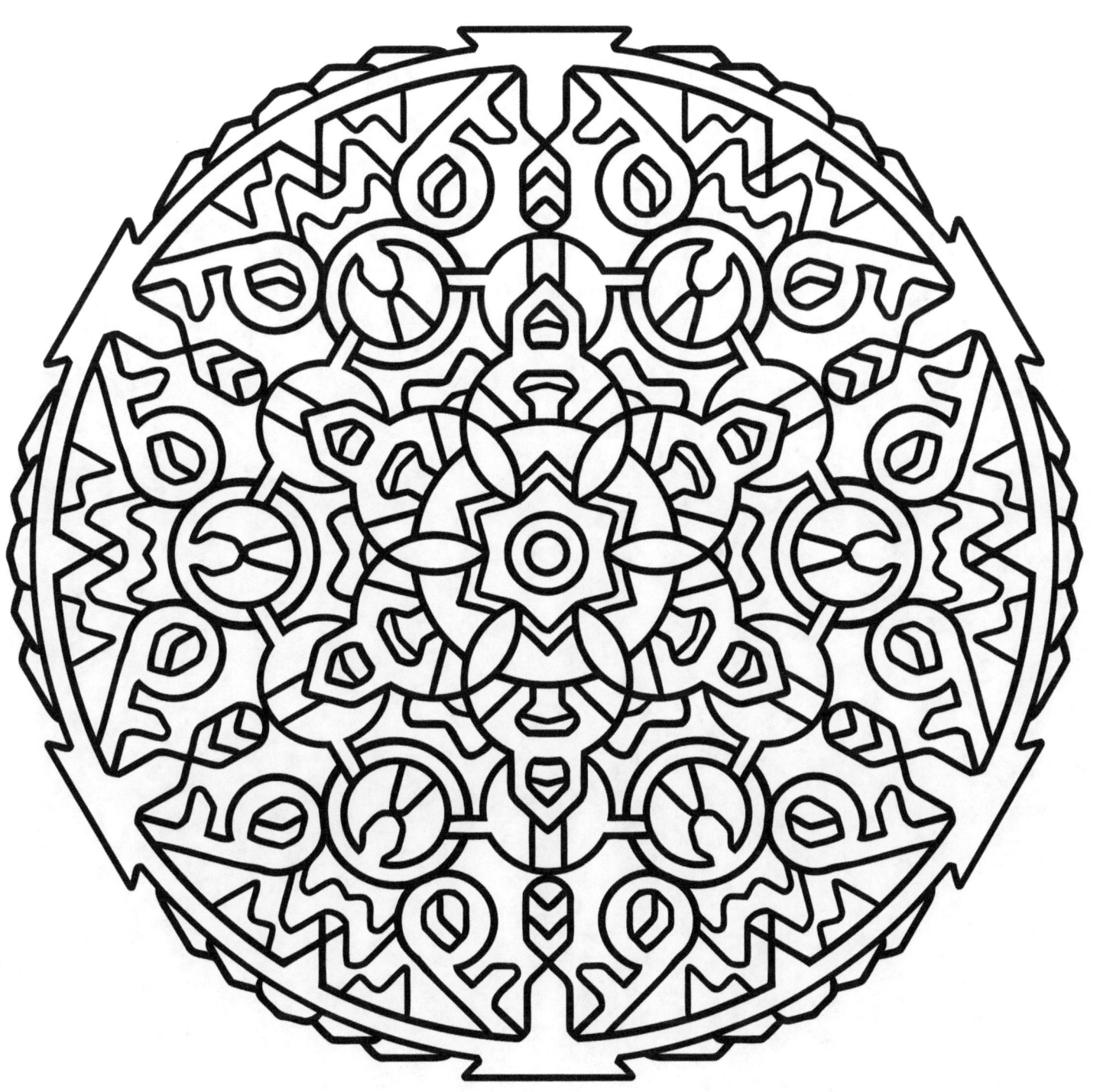

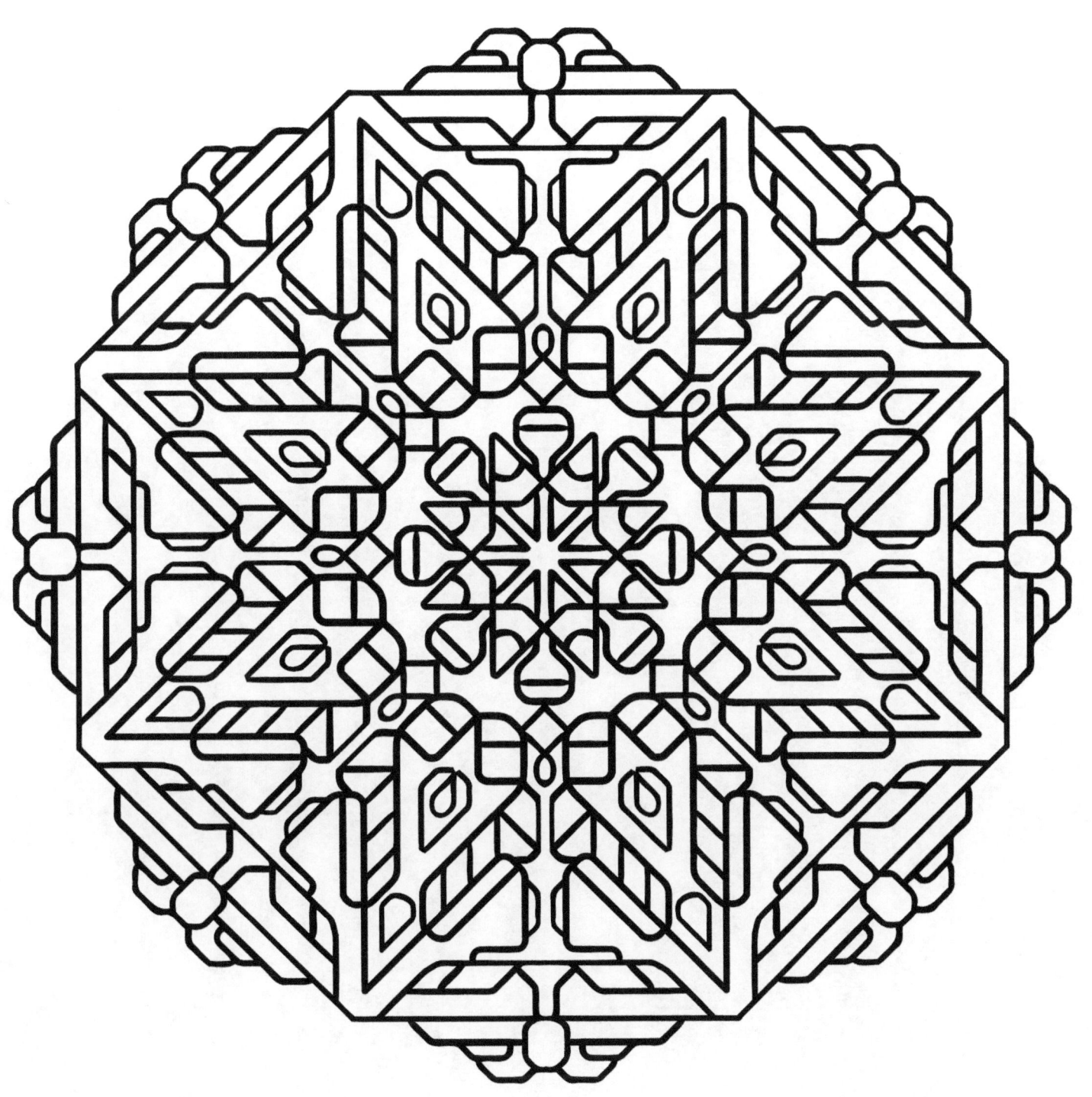

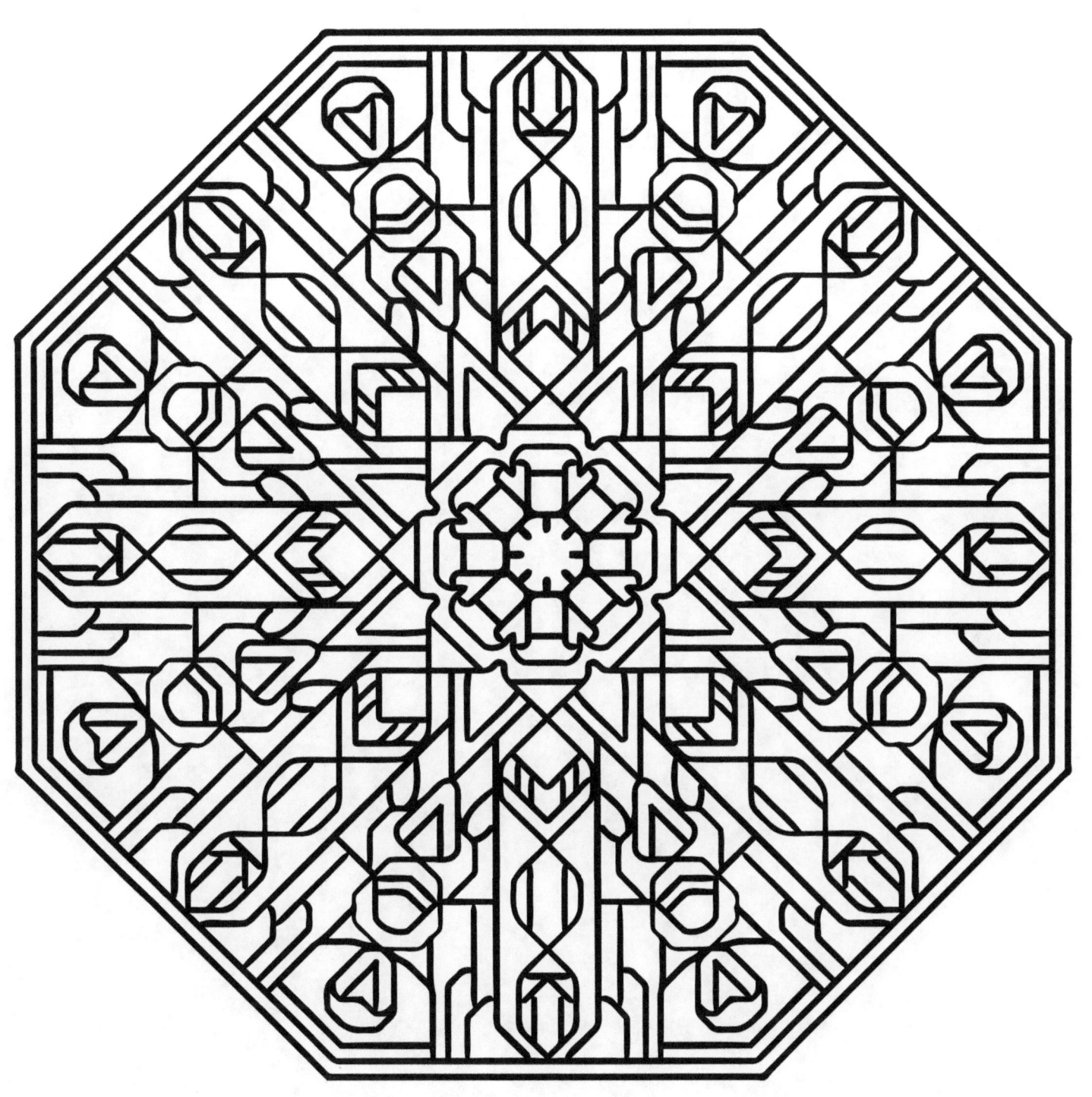

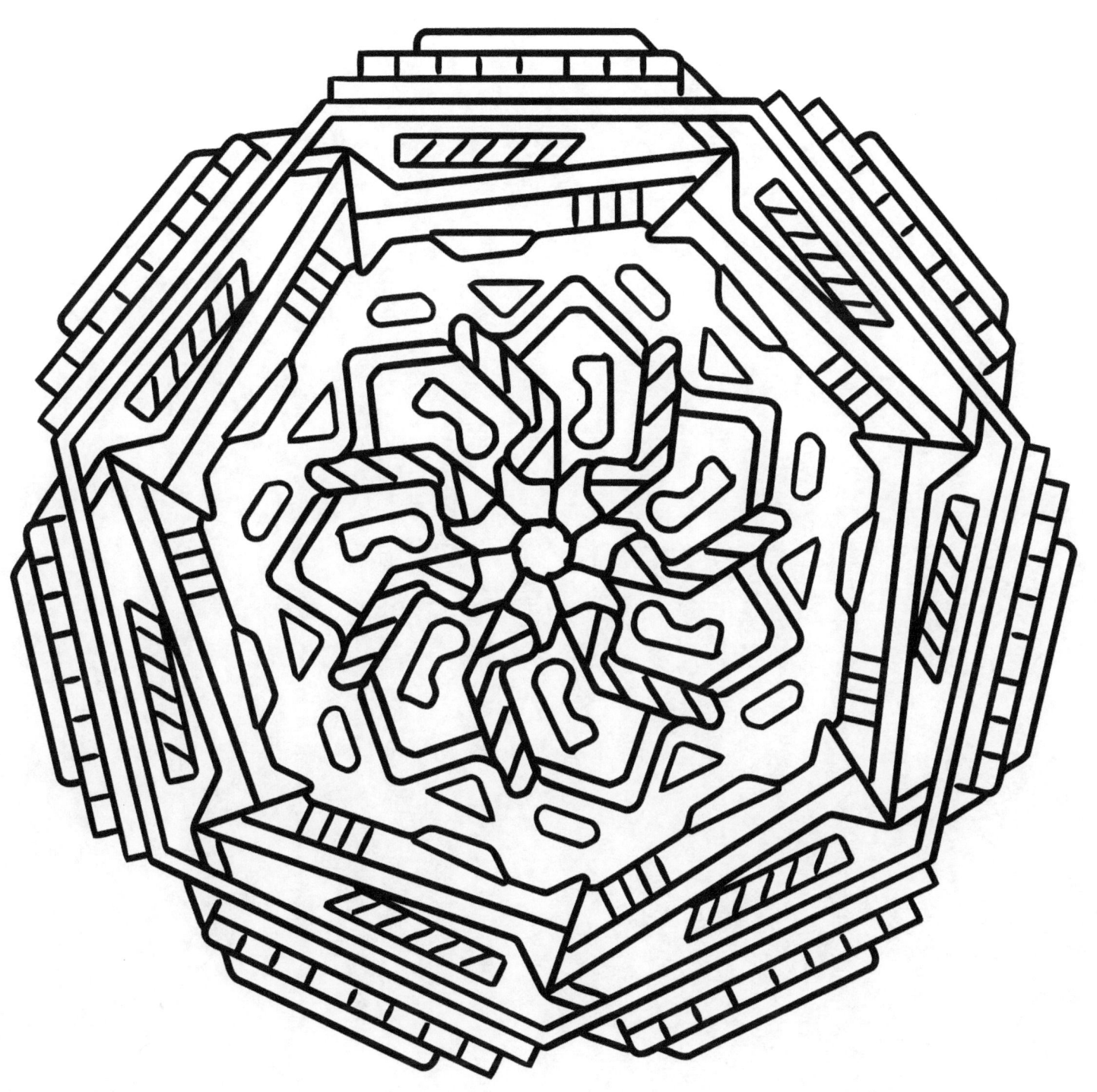

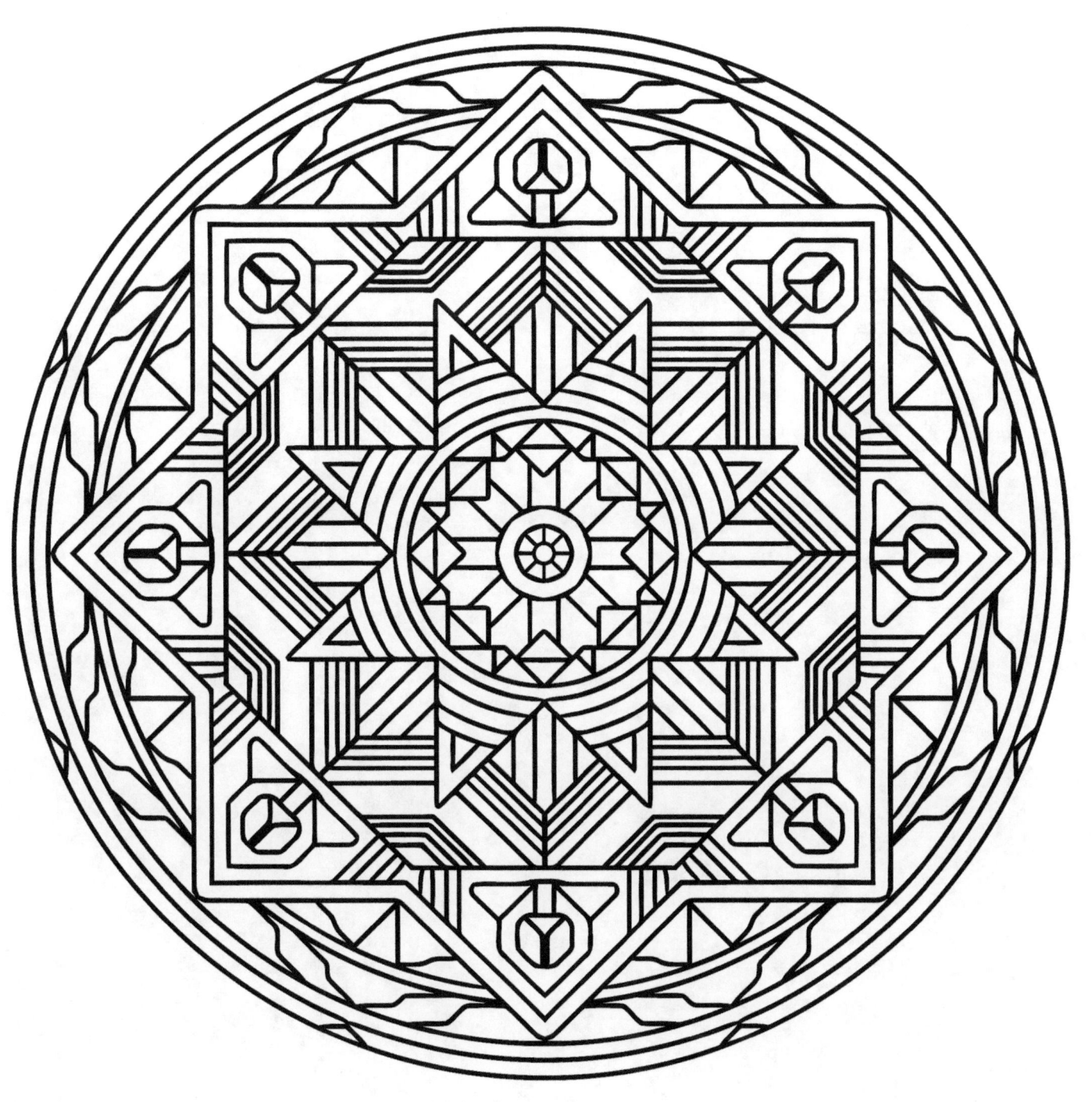

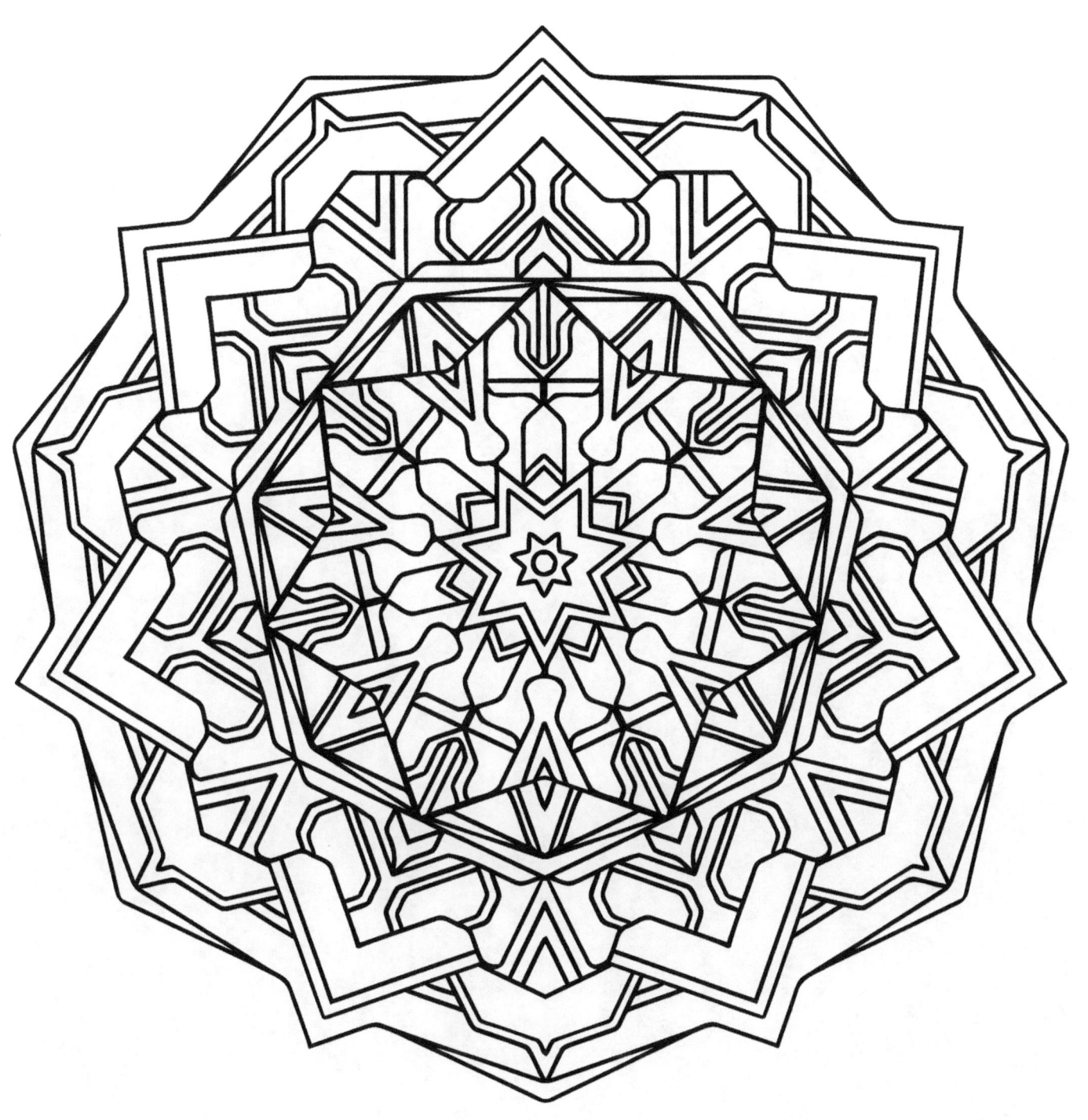

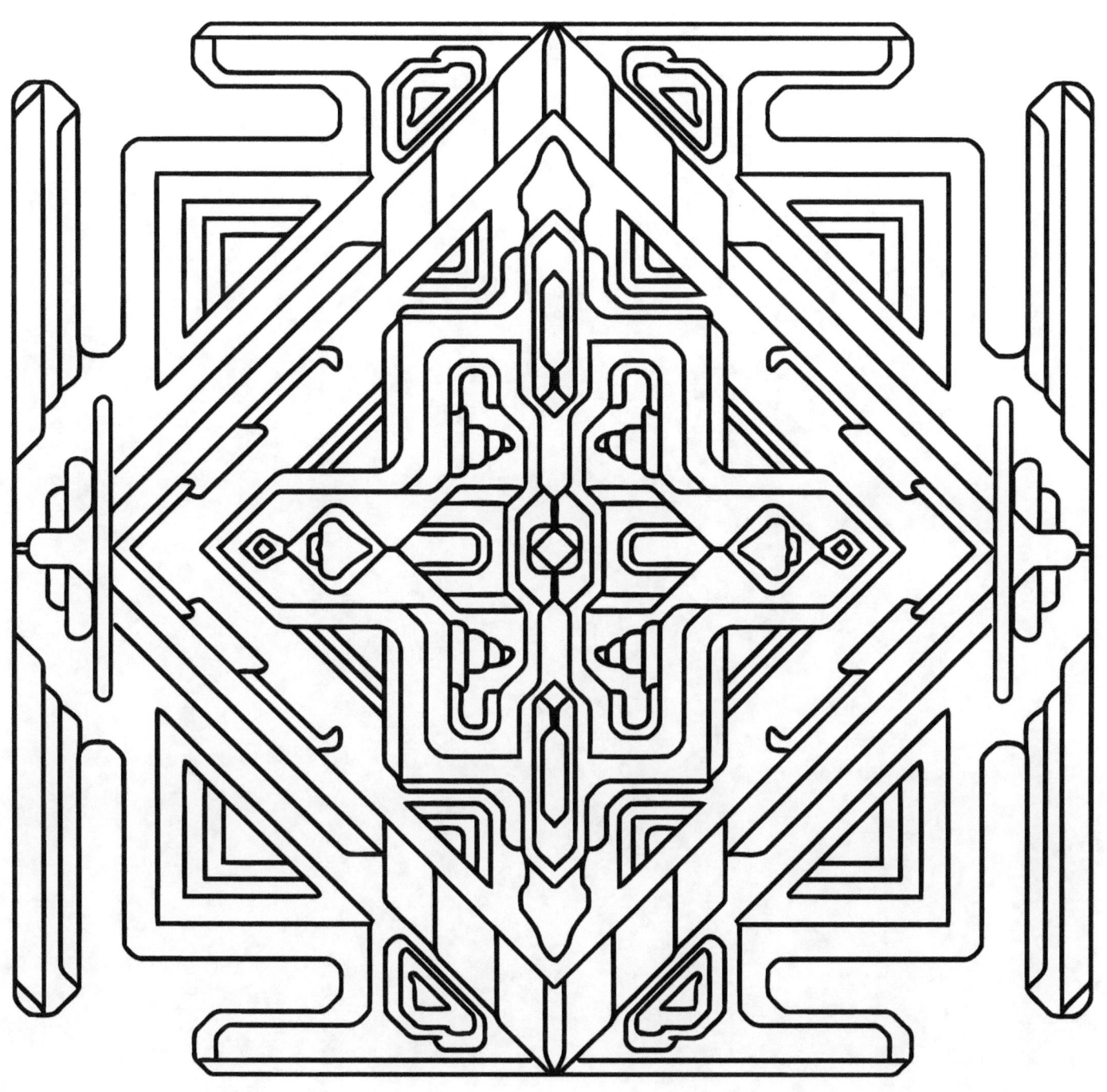

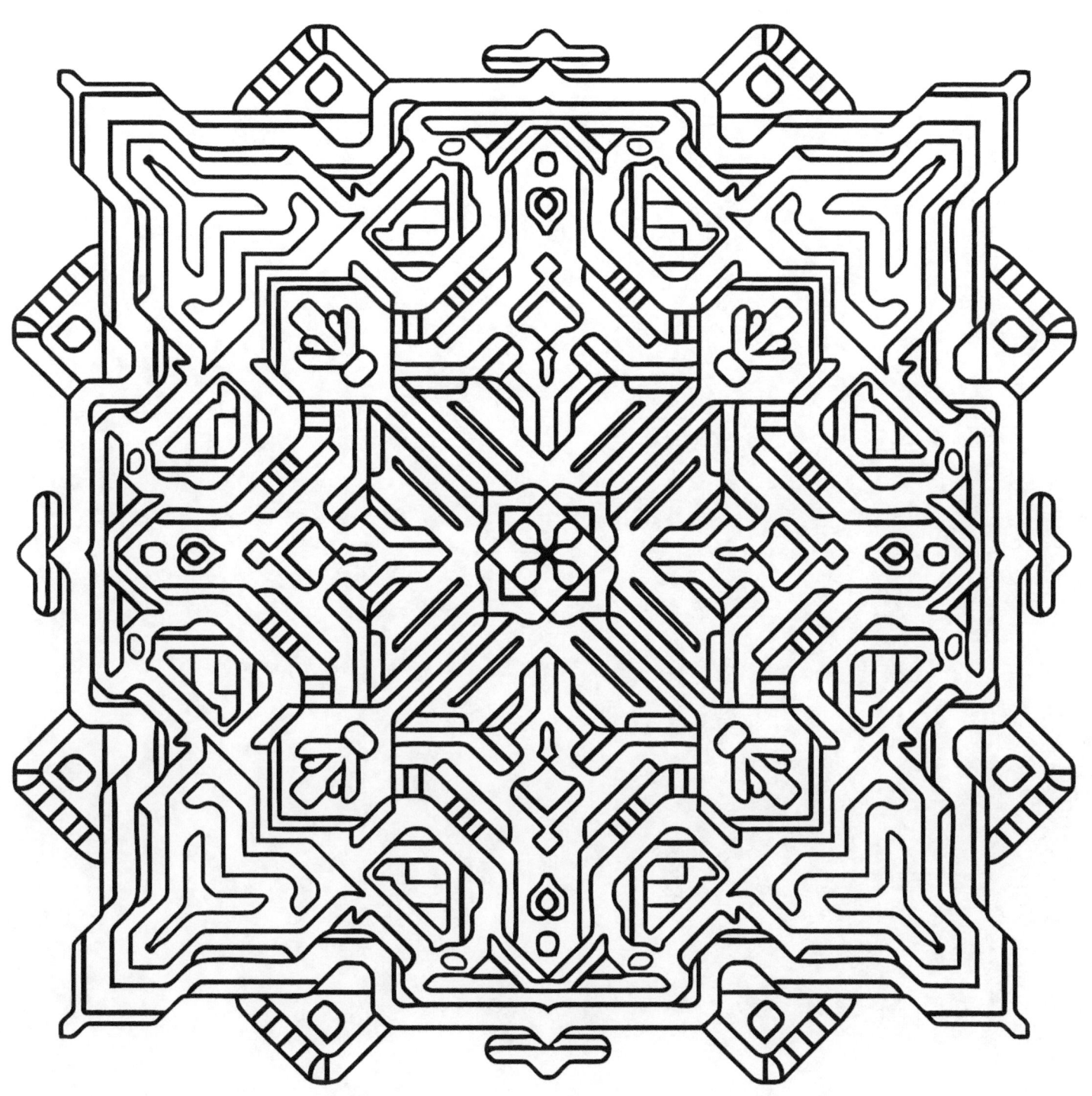

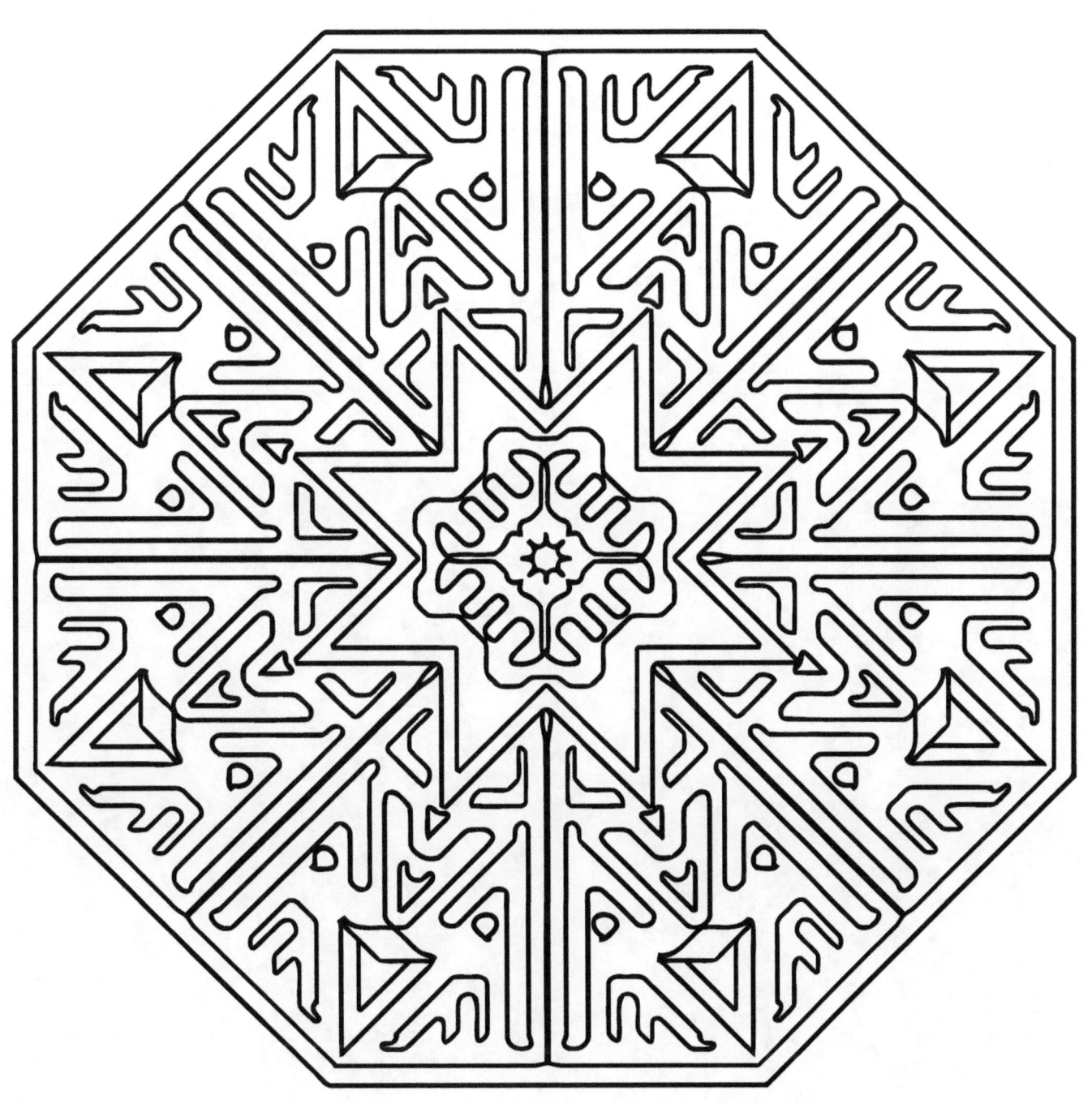

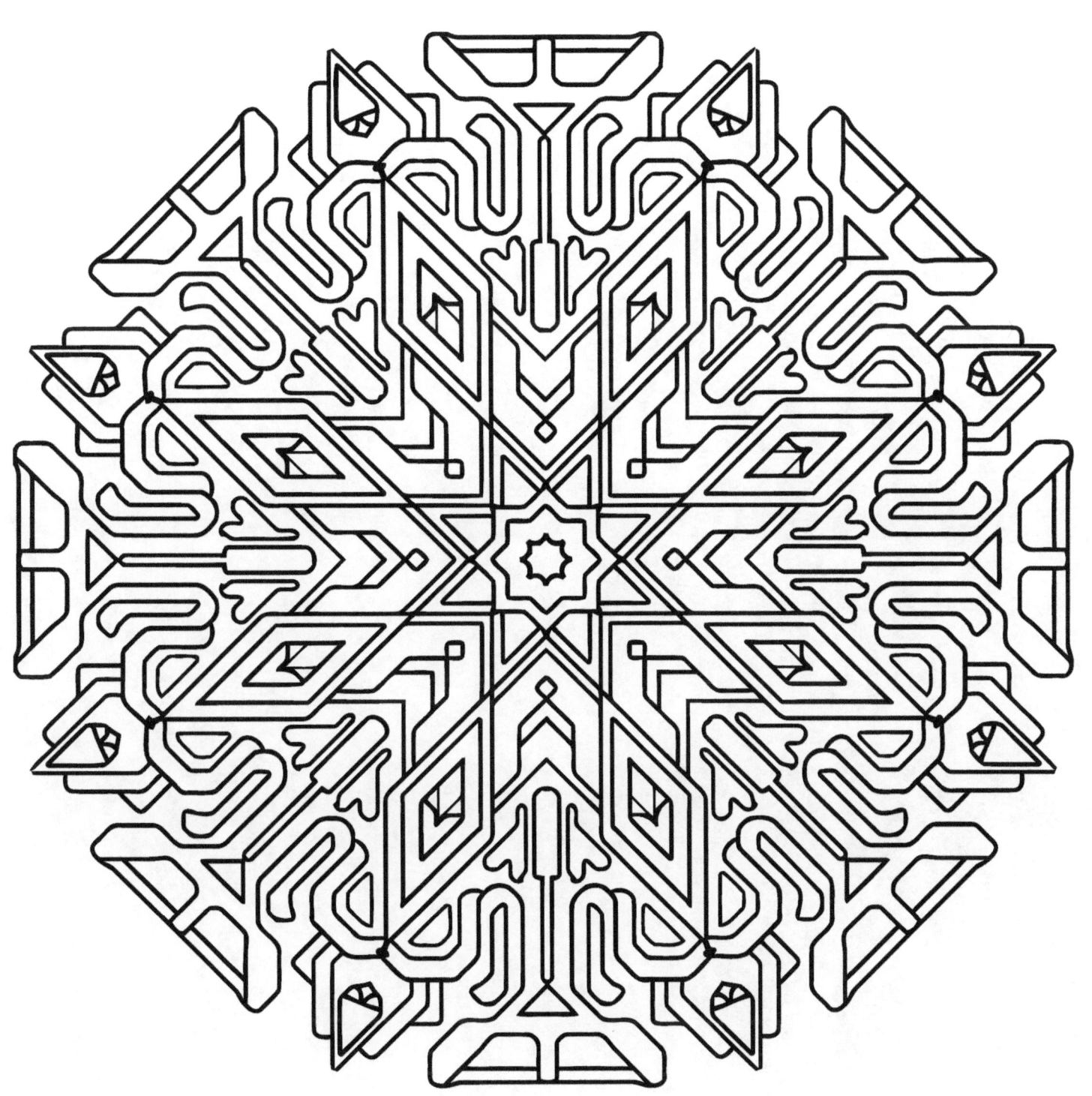

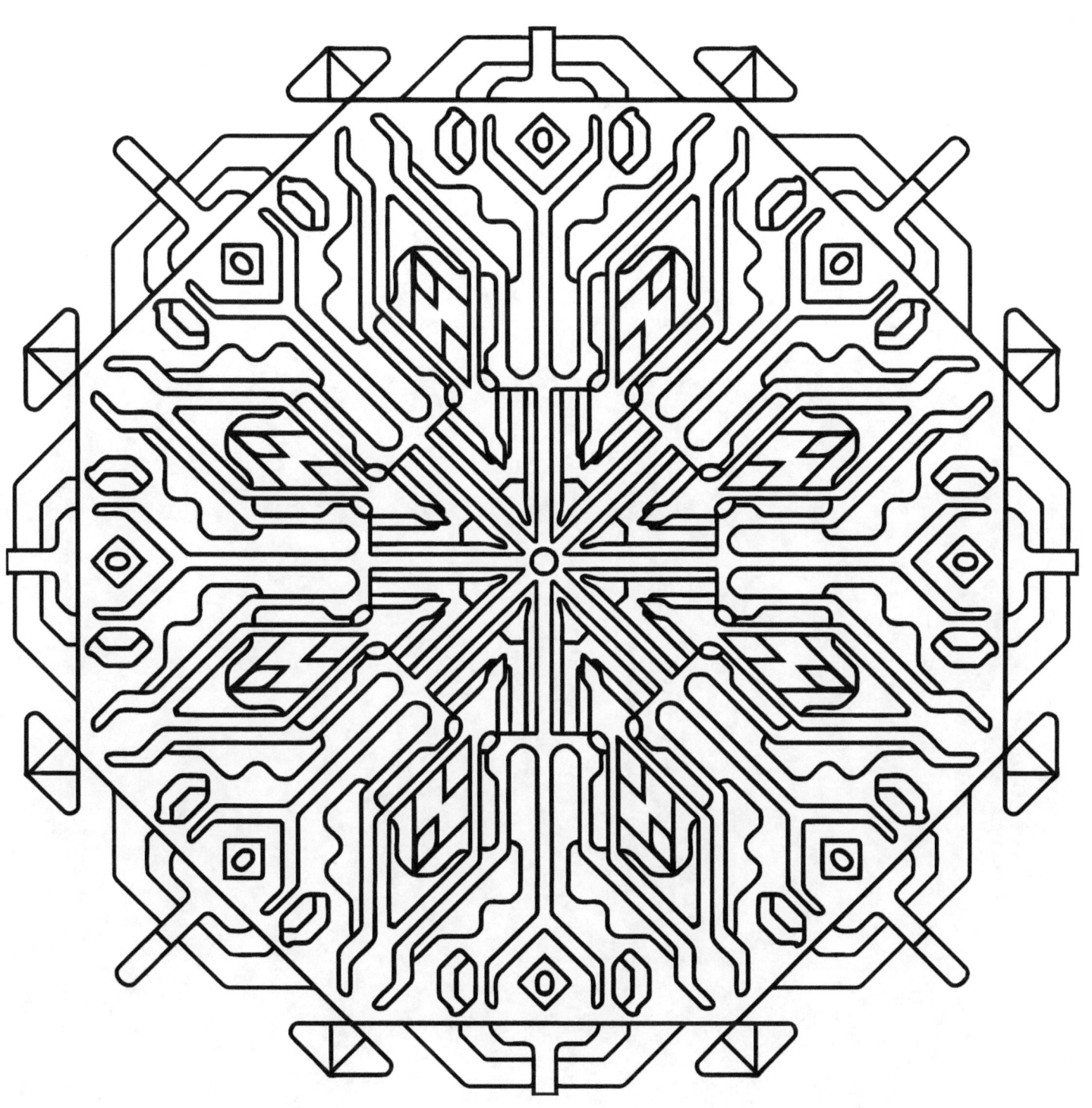

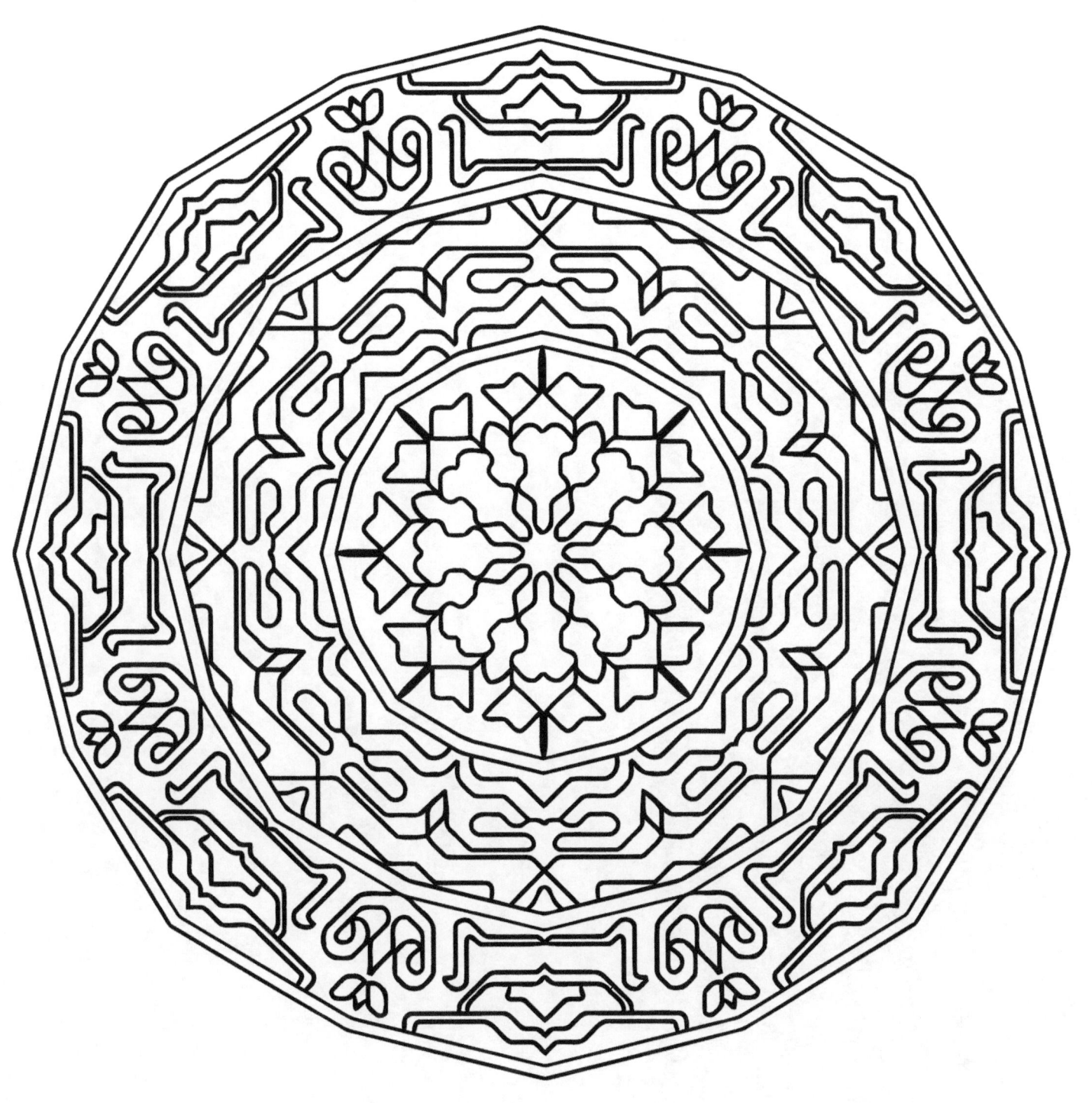

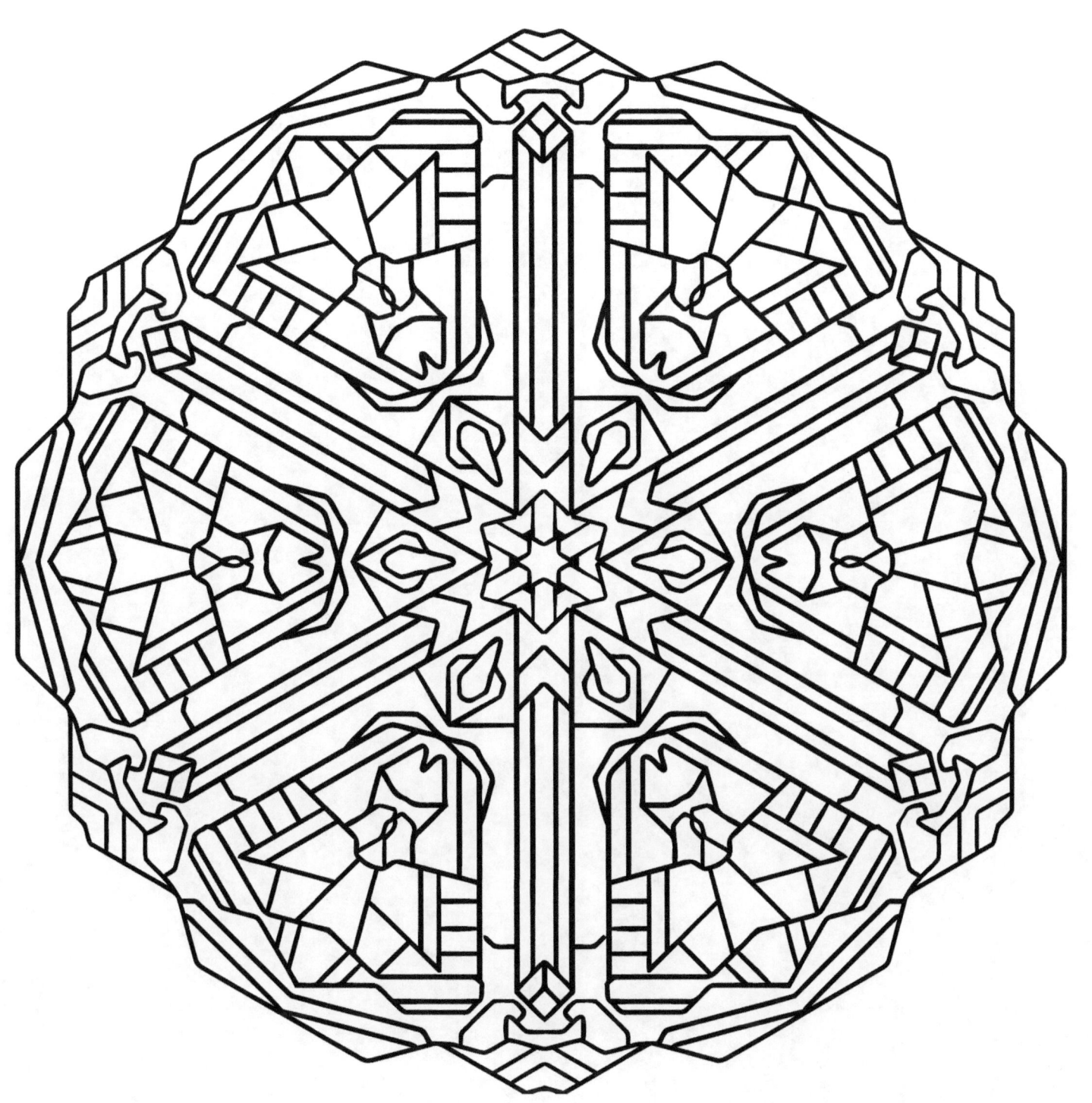

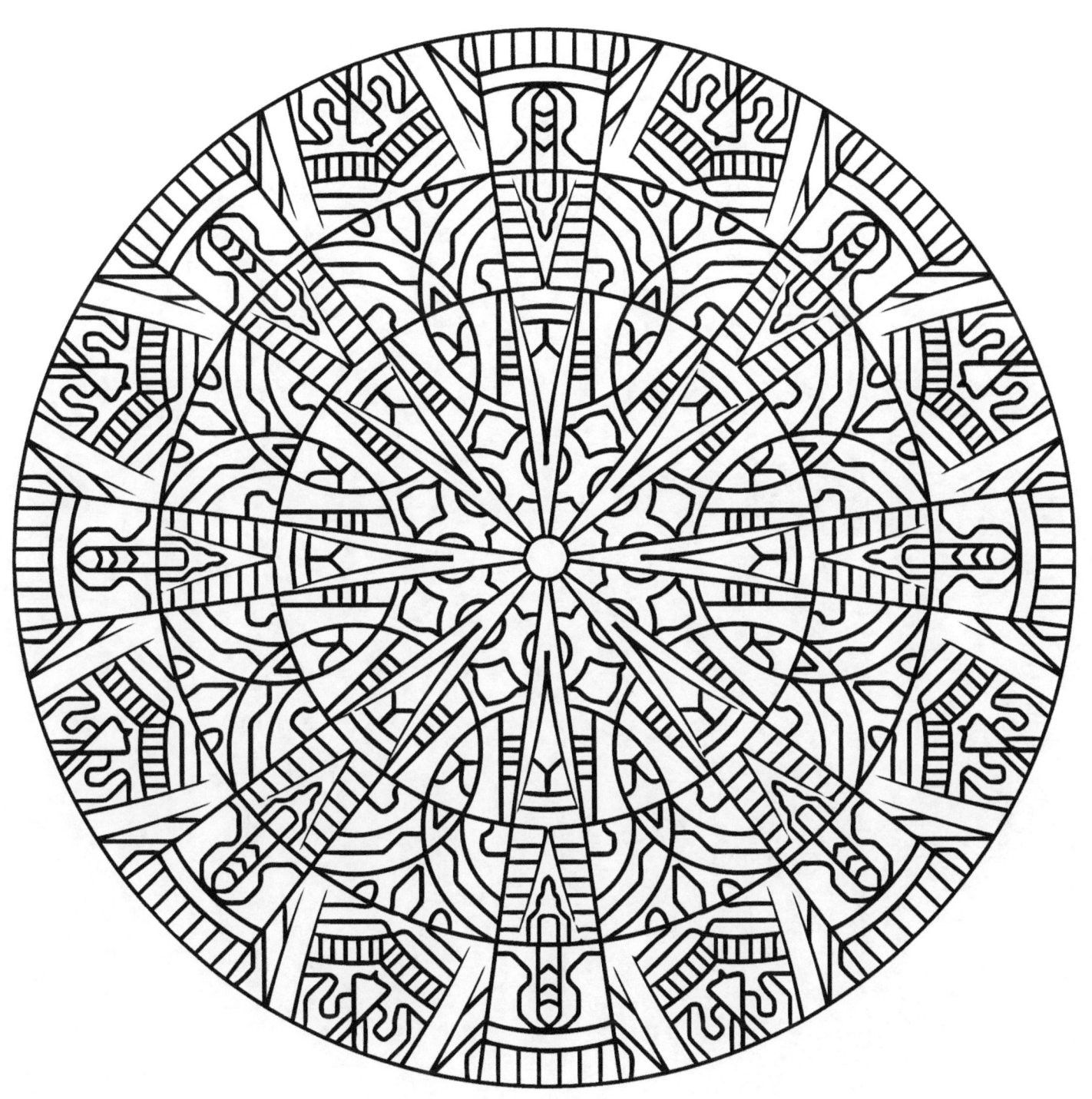

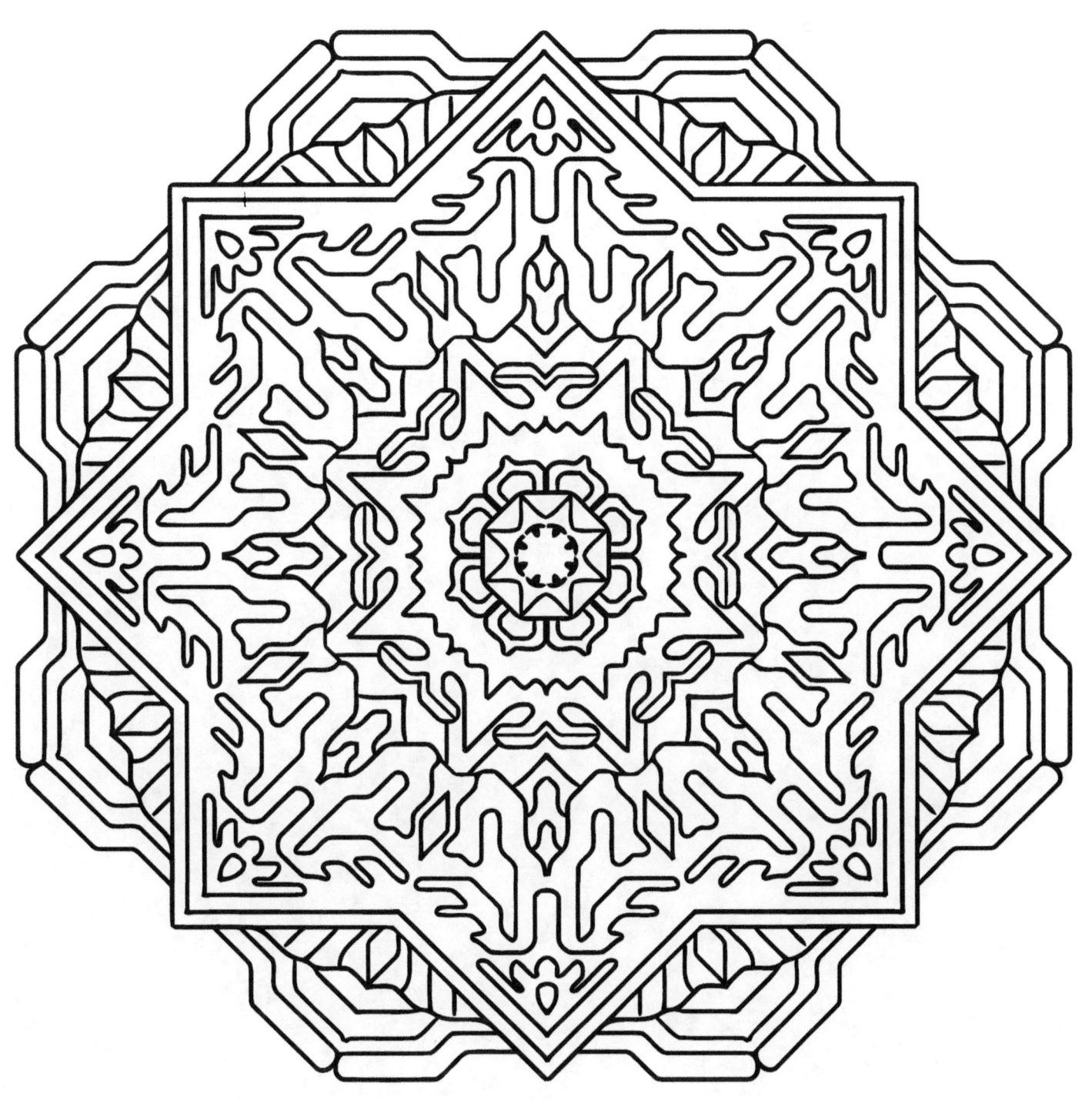

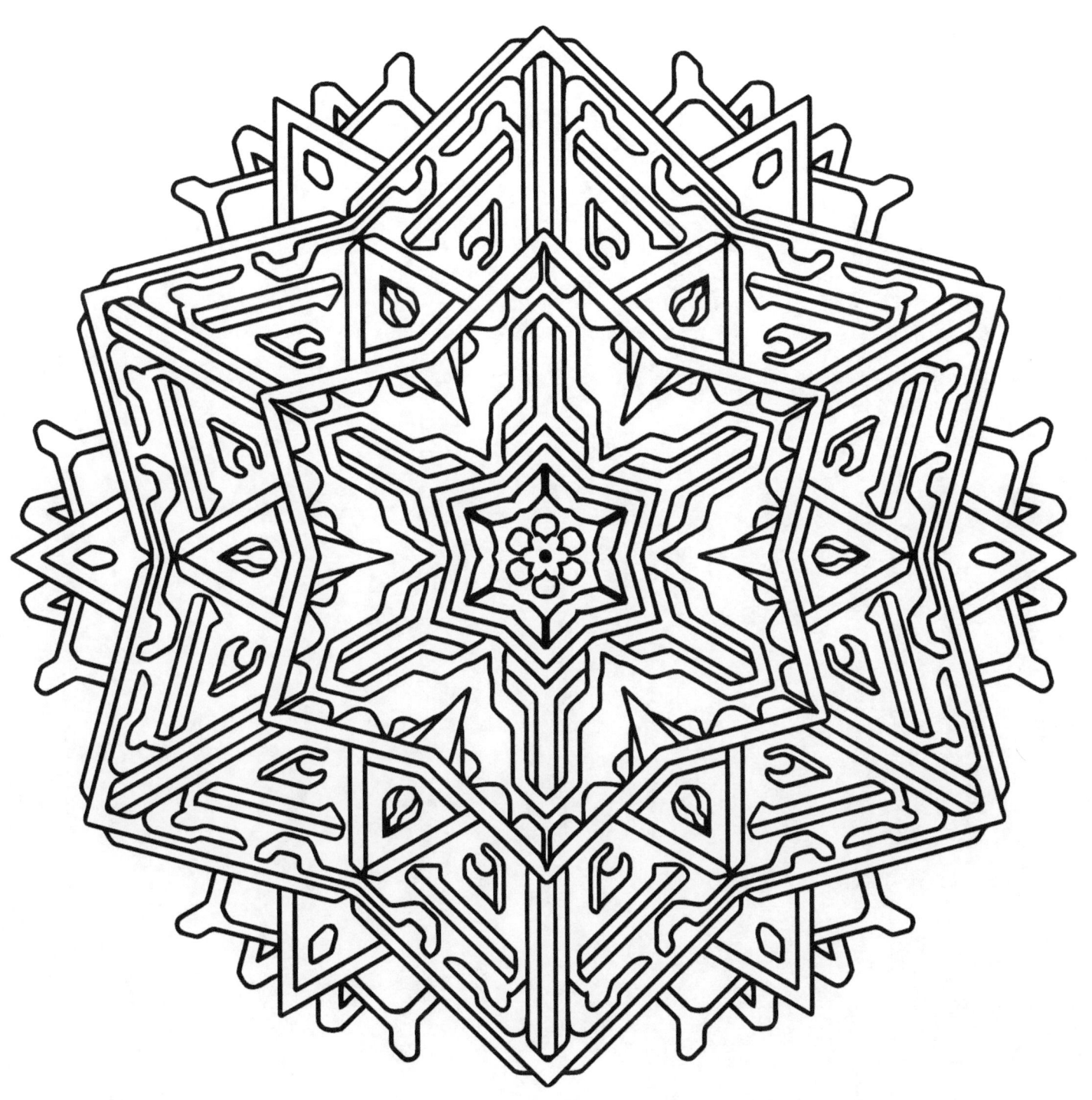

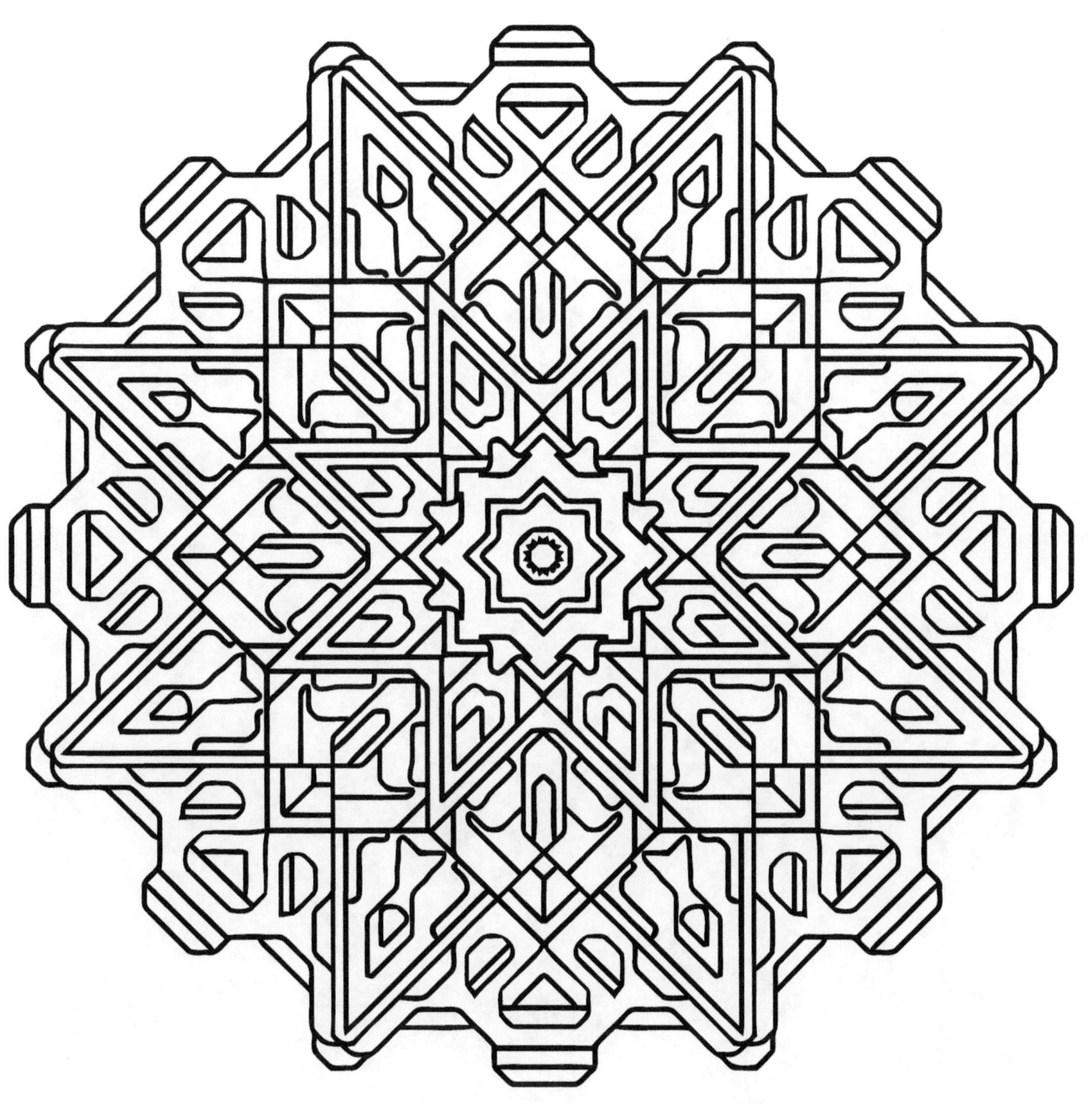

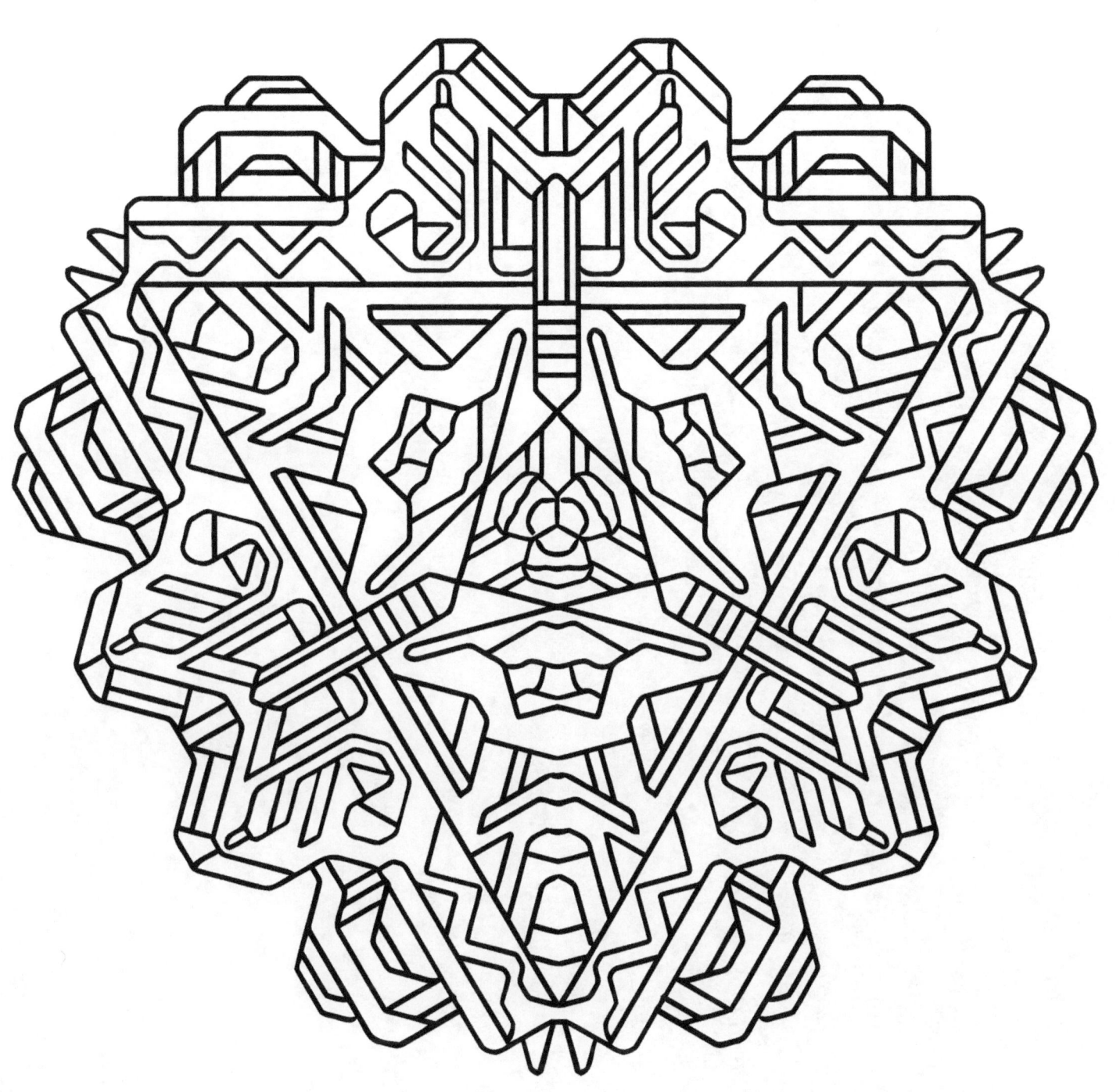

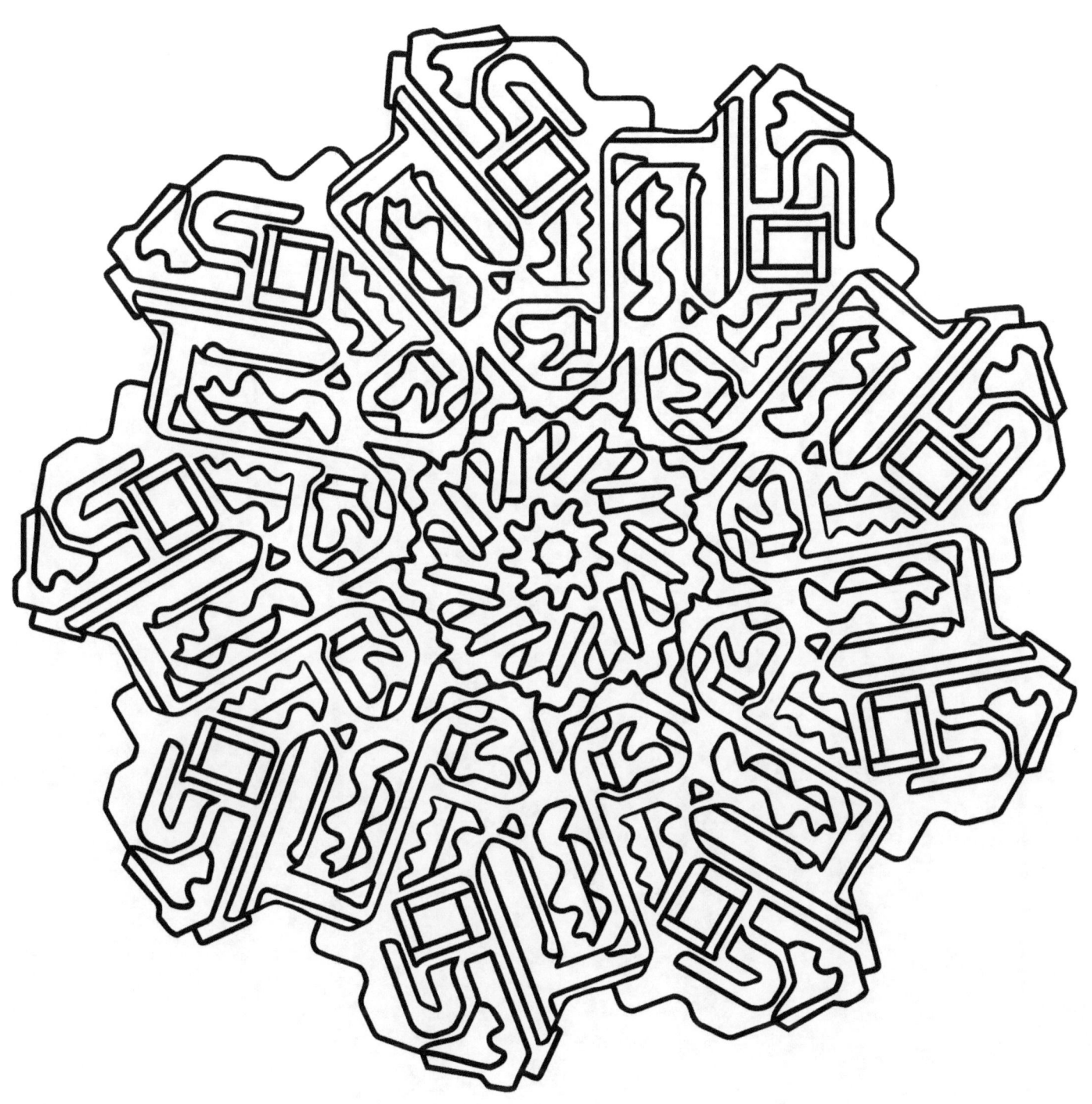

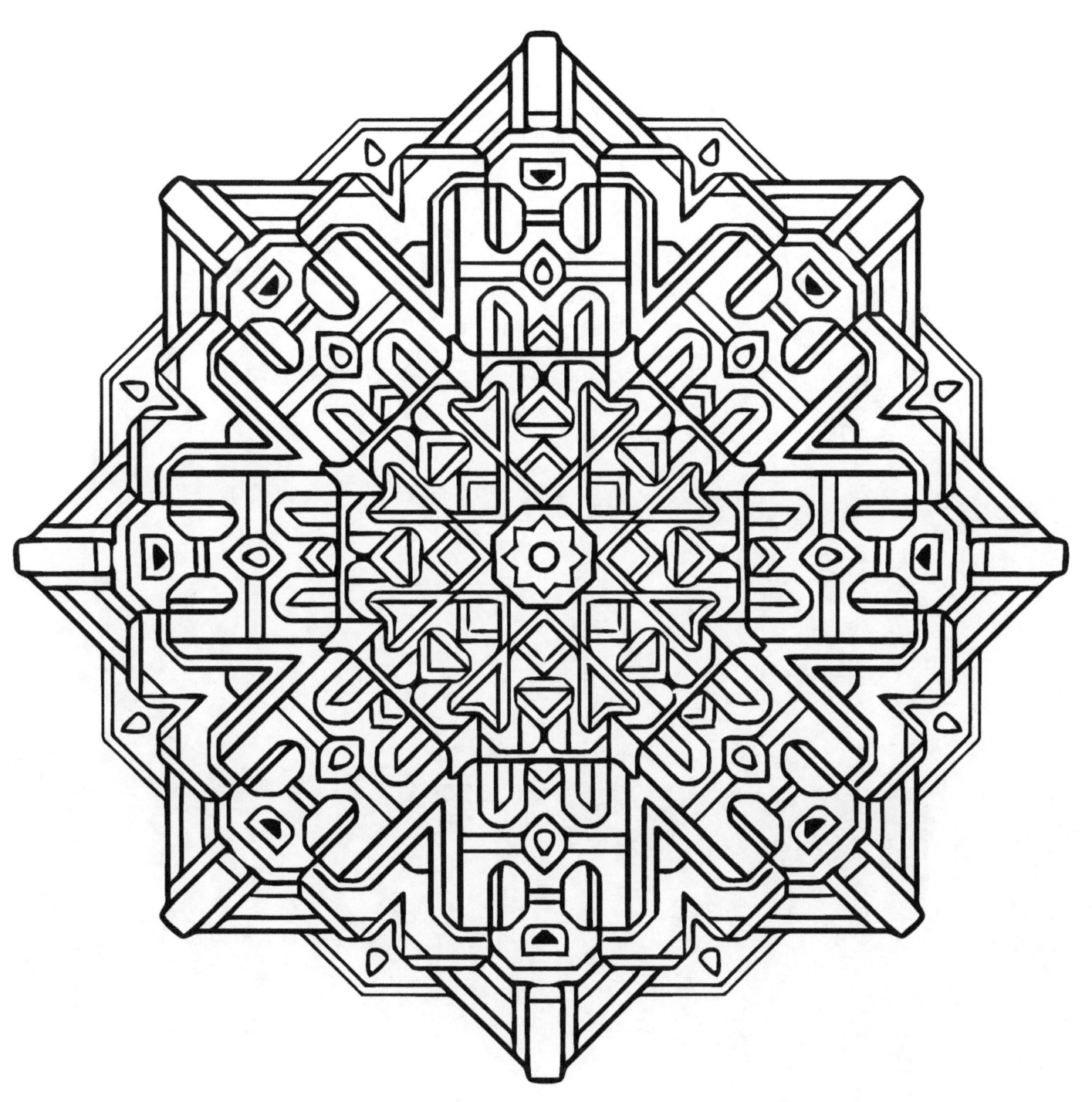

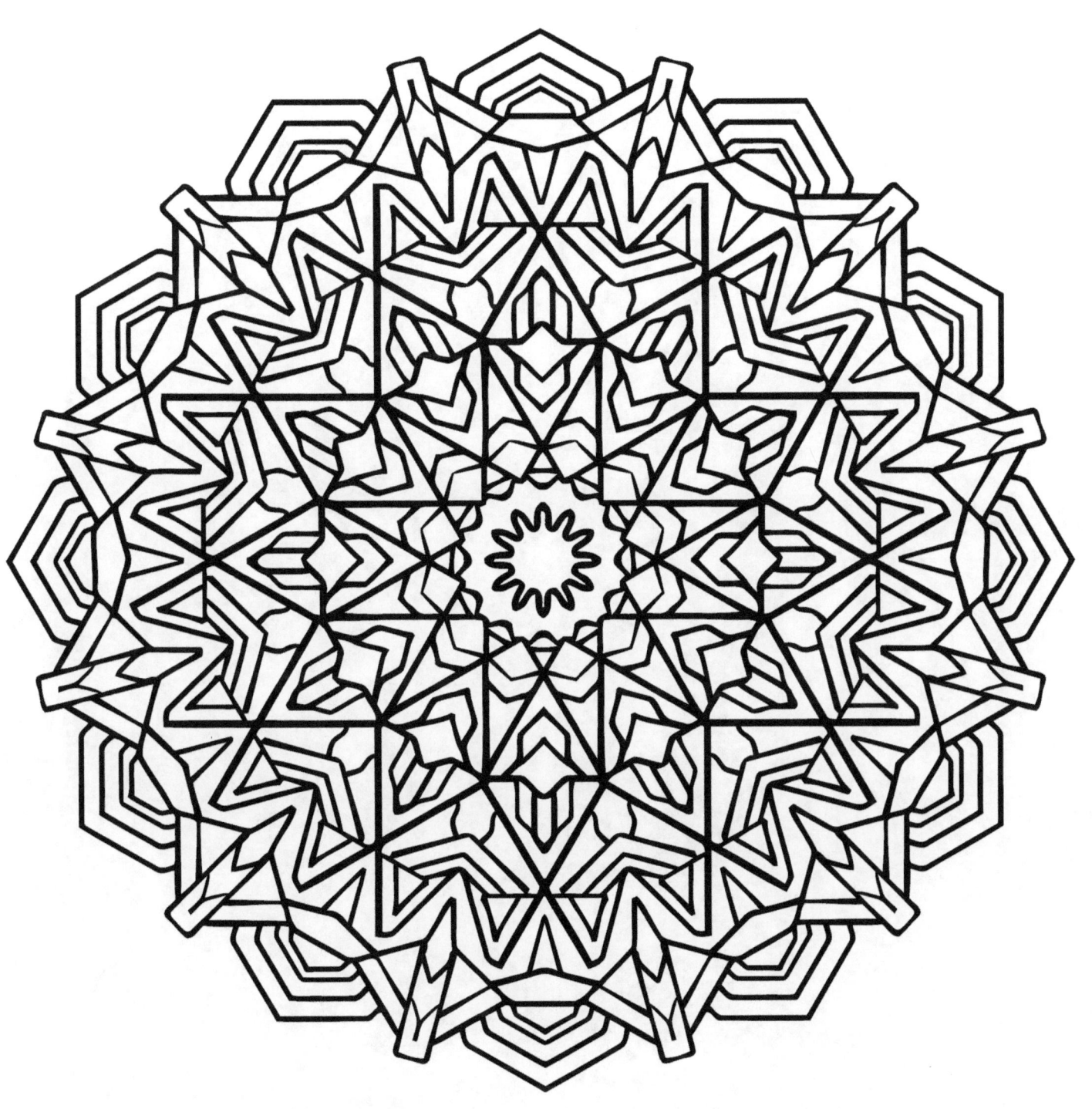

For more designs and upcoming books, please visit our facebook group at :

@coloringbooksandmandalas